THE
POSTAGE STAMP
KITCHEN GARDEN BOOK

THE POSTAGE STAMP KITCHEN GARDEN BOOK

Duane [G.] and Karen Newcomb

Adams Media Corporation
Holbrook, Massachusetts

Adams Media Corporation, ~~~~~~~~~~~~~~~~~~~~~~

ISBN: 1-58062-001-9

Printed in Canada.

J I H G F E D C B A

Library of Congress Cataloging-in-Publication Data
Newcomb, Duane G.
The postage stamp kitchen garden book / by Duane and Karen Newcomb.
p.   cm.
ISBN 1-58062-001-9
1. Vegetable gardening. 2. Organic gardening. I. Newcomb, Karen. II. Title.
SB324.3.N497   1998
635-dc21   97-43184
CIP

Product or brand names used in this book may be trademarks or registered trademarks. For readability, they may appear in initial capitalization or have been capitalized in the style used by the name claimant. Any use of these names is editorial and does not convey endorsement of or other affiliation with the name claimant. The publisher does not intend to express any judgment as to the validity or legal status of any such proprietary claims.

COVER ILLUSTRATION: Irena Roman
TEXT ILLUSTRATIONS: Barry Littmann

This book is available at quantity discounts for bulk purchases.
For information, call 1-800-872-5627 (in Massachusetts, 781-767-8100).

Visit our home page at http://www.adamsmedia.com

Contents

What Is a Postage Stamp Kitchen Garden?

A postage stamp kitchen garden is a small garden that puts the fresh ingredients that good cooks need at their fingertips when they need them. Kitchen gardens are very special places designed by, and for, people who love to cook and who are constantly looking for dishes that let them express their personalities. They are also for cooks who collect specialty recipes featuring hard-to-find ingredients such as poblano and chipotle chilies, cilantro, cumin, Italian parsley, and green onions.

These gardens are for those who would like the luxury of having eight or nine kinds of mints available, such as ginger mint, pineapple mint, or apple mint. Gourmet cooks may like to try some of the exotic melons, such as French Charentais or the Asian melons, Early Silver Line and Sprite. Kitchen gardens are also for cooks who specialize in vegetarian and light cooking, or salads, and for those who like to cook Italian, French, Oriental, Mexican, and Italian meals.

Unfortunately, many good cooks today complain that they are short on both time and garden space. The postage stamp kitchen garden solves both of these problems because it (1) produces tremendous amounts of vegetables in a small space using intensive techniques; (2) requires much less weeding, watering, and effort; (3) maintains ecological balance using intensive organic methods that create a vigorous, healthy vegetable garden; and (4) often combines in-ground gardens with containers. We know one cook whose kitchen garden consists of a window container planted with six types of basil. Another garden includes several patio containers plus 8 square feet of flowerbed space near the kitchen, with a 4-by-4-foot in-ground garden near the back door.

In short, postage stamp kitchen gardens are highly productive small gardens especially designed for good cooks everywhere who want their gardens to reflect the menus they serve and who aren't willing to settle for less than the best.

Chapter One

Planning Your Kitchen Garden

Good cooks usually plan their kitchen garden with menus and favorite dishes in mind. They indulge their whims with gardens designed to let them cook a variety of specialties: herb and garlic mashed potatoes, roasted tomato pasta salad, or a wide variety of Italian, French, Oriental, Mexican, and vegetarian dishes. A kitchen garden should become a testing ground for your ideas and recipes.

Good cooks know that a particular dish might need fresh basil or a cupful of tender young carrots. A favorite salad might consist of three different kinds of lettuce, red and yellow tomatoes, exotic greens, green and red sweet peppers, onions, and an herb or two.

Our neighbor is constantly conjuring up new ways to prepare food. She loves pasta salad and fixes it in many different ways, often using jalapeño chilies and the black beans that her family loves. To zip up the flavor even more, she might add bold seasonings such as cilantro or cumin. Another friend likes to eat healthy, so he concentrates on squashes, carrots, potatoes, and high-fiber foods such as beans. Other cooks who once shopped in ethnic markets for their authentic vegetables can now grow these same varieties in their own kitchen gardens.

What Do You Eat?

Before you rush out and plant a garden, spend a little time thinking about how you cook and how your family eats. Do you like salads, low-calorie cooking, pasta, or hearty chowders and stews? We don't care much for turnips, yet we love tomatoes and use them in almost everything. Our son hates turnips, rutabagas, Brussels sprouts, and spinach, so in our planning stage we often eliminate all of these vegetables, even if they are easy to grow.

After you make your choices, you can then select the number of plants you need by checking Table 1-1. Try new recipes that call for unfamiliar vegetables, and use a notebook to keep track of the vegetable varieties you've enjoyed.

To decide which herbs you'll need, look at the jars of dried herbs you already have in your kitchen. These are probably the ones you'll eventually want in your garden. We do not recommend that you plant everything the first year. Start with two or three herbs in your first kitchen garden, and add to them as you go along. You will also need to decide whether you want to plant herbs in with the vegetables or to have separate beds for them.

As you cook, you can also look at this the other way around. When Karen is making a hearty chicken soup, for instance, she frequently goes out into the garden with a basket to see what she can come up with to put into the pot. Often she comes back with rosemary, oregano, parsley, onions, celery, garlic, and carrots. Her soups and stews are always a tasty vegetable surprise.

What you find to eat in your garden also depends on the season. In some areas of the country, you can grow lettuce, broccoli, cabbage, tomatoes, cucumbers, and peppers all together during the summer. In the warmer areas, lettuce and other greens are grown in the spring and fall; tomatoes, cucumbers, squash, and similar vegetables are grown in the summer. Where

TABLE 1-1 NUMBER OF PLANTS PER PERSON			
VEGETABLE	**PLANTS PER PERSON**	**VEGETABLE**	**PLANTS PER PERSON**
Bean, snap	2–3	Melon	2
Bean, snap (pole)	1–2	Mustard	4–6
Bean (shell)	3–4	Okra	1–2
Beet	10–20	Onion	10–30
Brussels sprouts	1	Parsnip	10
Cabbage	2	Pea, snap	3–4
Cabbage, Chinese	2–3	Pepper	1–2
Carrot	30–50	Potato	1–2
Cauliflower	6–10	Pumpkin	1
Celeriac	1	Radish	20–60
Celery	1–2	Rutabaga	3–6
Collards	2–5	Salsify	2–10
Corn, sweet	5–6	Shallot	4–10
Cucumber	1–2	Spinach	3–7
Eggplant	1	Spinach, New Zealand	5
Garlic	4	Squash, summer	1
Horseradish	1–2	Squash, winter	2
Kale	2–3	Sweet potato	2
Kohlrabi	4–6	Swiss chard	1
Leek	6–10	Tomato	2
Lettuce, head	3–4	Tomato, paste	3
Lettuce, leaf	2–4	Turnip	8–15
		Watermelon, bush	1

we live in California, we can grow all types of stir-fry greens and snow peas all winter long. Karen loves this bonus growing season because it gives her the chance to try recipes that are different from our favorite summer ones. We'll get to the seasonal differences in vegetables as we go along.

What Else Would You Like?

Consider also what else you want out of a garden. We often plant flowers among the vegetables, partially because some of them repel insects and nematodes, or they have beneficial effects for the other vegetables. Edible flowers add color and taste to salads, and some flowers have such sweet scents they attract bees and hummingbirds to the garden.

Favorite Edible Flowers

Many cooks say that nasturtiums are an essential part of their kitchen garden. Nasturtiums are often used in salads to add a peppery taste and color. They are also used as a garnish on many other dishes. Fastidious cooks like them because of the variety of colors they can add. *Creamsicle* has petals with a swirled pastel that highlights a deep red throat, *Peach Melba* has yellow petals accented with raspberry, *Moonlight* has pale yellow blossoms, and *Sungold* has deep butter yellow petals.

You can select from 1-foot compact types to 6-foot climbing/trailing varieties. Plant after all danger of frost is past. Nasturtiums thrive when their roots are cool and moist. Plants that get too much water have large leaves but few flowers.

The edible flower petals of calendula are used in ales and for food coloring. These plants also make a colorful ornamental that brightens the corner of any garden. In warm areas, they will bloom and be available all winter long.

Plants that Attract Butterflies

Some kitchen gardens are planted to attract butterflies, birds, and beneficial insects. Butterflies seem to add magic to the garden, especially when a swallowtail or a painted lady lights on a nearby flower. Butterfly gardens need plenty of flowers for nectar and food plants for caterpillars. Most caterpillars confine themselves to one plant family or one specific plant. Some butterfly plants are bee balm, coreopsis, morning glory, verbena, and zinnia. Shrubs such as the butterfly bush, fruit trees, mock orange, and spirea also attract butterflies.

W. Atlee Burpee offers a butterfly bird garden in their catalog. Here is what they suggest:

Silvia coccinea	Cosmos
Snapdragon	Zinnia
Blue boy	Lady in red
Sensation white	Red rocket
Cornflower	Marigold

Plants that Attract Hummingbirds

Birds also make a garden come alive, but at certain times of the year, they can also eat everything as soon as it pops out of the ground. As a result, when we plant early in the spring—when birds seem to be the hungriest—we have to plant most crops under row covers. If you are a bird lover, concentrate on hummingbirds: they make for good natural insect control since they regularly pick off insects. They also gather nectar from flowers with their needlelike bill and long tongues. To attract them you might want to set out one or two hummingbird feeders or add their favorite plants to your garden. Some suggestions are columbine, coral bells, sage, fuchsia, monkey flower, gilia, honeysuck-le, or butterfly bush.

Orchard Mason Bees

With the present pollination crisis caused by infestations of honey bees, Orchard Mason bees help fill the void. The Orchard Mason bees are small black bees that do not harm humans or pets. These native bees do not dwell in hives. When the weather warms up in early spring, the bees emerge from their holes.

After they mate, the females begin to make their nests and gather pollen and nectar from the spring blossoms. Gardeners can make their own nesting blocks out of 1- or 2-foot-long ponderosa pine or Douglas fir pieces. Simply drill a number of holes in the block and hang it around the garden.

Attracting Bugs to Your Garden

It is possible to lure insects that prey on vegetables pests, pollinate plants, and build soil. Start with a 10-gallon plastic tub, which you can find at hardware stores. Drill holes in the tub's bottom to provide drainage. Fill the tub with a mixture of planting soil and compost.

Now, include six to eight of these plants, which are rich in pollen: nico-tonia, autumn sage, lemon queen, catmint, blue daze, verbena, silver thyme, lavender, cosmos, nasturtium, and trailing rosemary. Water several times a week, and feed with fish emulsion on a weekly basis. Ask at your local nursery where to purchase them.

Seed Shopping by Catalog

Garden catalogs are essential tools for planning your kitchen garden. There are probably several hundred vegetable, flower, and herb catalogs.

Many of them have unique personalities and a seed selection you'll never find on the seed racks.

Horticultural Enterprises caters to pepper afficionados; it offers dozens of varieties. Tomato Growers Supply is entirely devoted to tomatoes. Shepherd's Garden Seeds and The Cook's Garden give priority to gourmet and specialty varieties. Many catalogs offer planting tips. Some even offer recipes.

Before you start your garden, we suggest you send for some of the catalogs listed in the Appendix. This is one of our favorite preplanning chores every year. It gives us a chance to select new and different varieties that we really want to try.

Other Considerations

Your kitchen garden will need to be defined by the number of hours you're willing to spend each week in your garden, how much money you can afford to put into your garden, the space you have available, how your kitchen garden fits into your yard, and what site makes the most sense. You'll also have to decide whether you're going to garden at ground level or in raised beds and whether you want to include a special garden for the kids. Here's a checklist:

1. What do I really want to grow?
2. Do I want a combination in-ground and container kitchen garden?
3. How big should I make my garden?
4. How much time do I have to spend each week?
5. Can I integrate my kitchen garden into my landscaping?
6. Do I want raised beds?

7. Do I need to grow my garden against a fence to support my vine plants?
8. Do I want to garden vertically?
9. Does pocket gardening make sense in my yard?
10. Do I want to grow enough vegetables to freeze or can?

Time and Money

Unless you're retired, most people are short on time. If you have a job and small children, you may only have an hour or two a week to spend in the garden. If you don't have to weed or water as much, you'll have more time for other activities, which is a consideration for a busy family or a couple. The less time you have to spend gardening, the smaller you need to make your kitchen garden. Everyone knows that the couple who rushes out and plants the entire backyard in plants winds up spending every spare moment just keeping up with it.

Gardening can be extremely expensive, or it can cost practically nothing. You can, for instance, buy garden compost or make your own. You can buy $42 pruners or $6 ones, pay $46 for pliant pants or garden in a pair of old jeans. You may want to splurge on kneeling pads, garden vests, and other gardening accessories—the choice belongs to you.

We feel that it pays to start small, spend a modest amount the first year, and then decide how much you can afford and want to spend on your garden as you go along.

What Kind of Garden?

You need to think of your kitchen garden as a very special place. It can be as small as four or five 8-inch pots on a kitchen windowsill or as large a plot as you can conveniently squeeze into the backyard.

Next, you need to answer some questions. Do you want to plant a few vegetables in your flower beds? Do you intend to put the garden in the middle of the backyard? How much container gardening do you want to do?

When you have answered these questions, make a sketch of your lot and house and look for possibilities. Consider spots that get sun. How about the back corners near the fence, or the side yard? Would you have 4 or 5 feet of flower bed space, or side-by-side beds that are 3 feet wide and perhaps 25 feet long? Our favorite size is the 4-by-4-foot bed, either grouped in three or four beds or all by itself.

Karen has a 4-foot bed that produces large quantities and more varieties of vegetables than I ever thought possible. Her Mexican garden overflowed with a 6-foot caged tomatillo plant, four Roma paste tomato plants, two Anaheim pepper plants, two Fresno peppers, one Tokantotsume hot cherry pepper plant, and cilantro. She even planted two Golden Bell sweet peppers, one Cardinal red pepper, and one Globe basil. At mid-season, her garden looked like a jungle, and after the first hundred tomatoes, I stopped counting.

Wide Beds, Not Rows

We always attempt to get the greatest number of vegetables possible out of the smallest space possible. To do this, we urge you to give up row gardening and plant all the way across the bed with the intensive method. This way you can cheat a bit on space; just plant at the same spacing in all directions as recommended on the seed package. As the plants mature, the overlapping leaves allow you to spend less time on such garden chores as weeding and watering. We've gardened the intensive way for more than twenty years and now feel it only makes sense to mass plant in a small area.

How about Raised Beds?

If you have poor, relatively unfertile soil, you may want to build raised beds from railroad ties or 12-by-2-inch redwood planks. Bring in loam, or create a better soil in your garden by combining your present soil with lots of organic material. However, if you have hot summers and sandy soil, raised beds will heat up early and dry out quickly. Under these conditions, you will probably want to garden at ground level.

If you are in a wheelchair, you can still garden. Raised beds at wheelchair working height make it possible for people with disabilities to garden in limited space (Figure 1-1).

Finally, you will need to fence your garden if you have deer or rabbits nearby or other animals. To deter rabbits, you need a 1-inch mesh fence. For deer, a 7- or 8-foot-high chicken wire fence is necessary.

All of these considerations will be covered in more detail in later chapters.

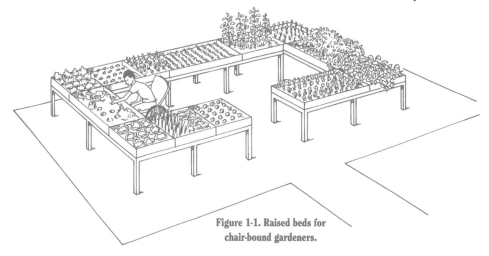

Figure 1-1. Raised beds for chair-bound gardeners.

Pocket Gardens

Short on garden space? Instead of thinking about conventional gardening, think in terms of using the pocket space scattered here and there around the yard. Pack a few beans, carrots, peppers, and tomatoes in between a garage and fenced property lines. Fan-shaped trellises in half barrels support cucumbers, while a small planter box on the patio can serve as an herb garden.

Up in the Air

In the planning stage, you need to consider using the space above your garden. Pocket gardeners also go crazy climbing the walls with beans, squash, melons, pumpkins, and cucumbers. These fruits and vegetables and other vining crops take up tremendous ground space, too much for most small kitchen gardens. When you use the space above the garden, you can produce large amounts of produce in a surprisingly small area.

The larger fruit must be supported as it begins to mature. Consider support frames, wire cages, folding wooden cages, A-frames, posts, and tripods (Figures 1-2 through 1-5).

Practical Solutions

Many people simply put their garden in the wrong place and regret it from then on. Here are some things you need to consider.

Figure 1-2. A drying rack can be the perfect frame for vertical gardening.

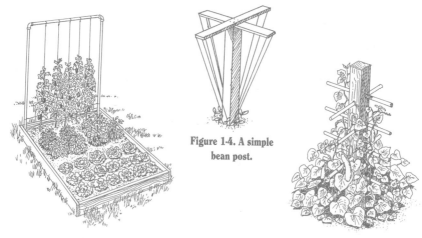

Figure 1-4. A simple
bean post.

Figure 1-3. Plastic pipe frames at
the north end of a garden.

Figure 1-5. A cucumber pole.

- Keep your garden away from trees. Vegetables such as corn and tomatoes (and other warm-season crops) need at least 8 hours of full sun a day. Lettuce and carrots (and the cool-season crops) thrive in a little shade, especially in mid-summer, but trees compete for nutrients from the soil in a circle as far out as the tree's branches. Plants within this circle often do poorly.

- Avoid low wet areas that are slow to dry in the spring, or areas that have a serious weed problem. If you garden on a slope, terrace the slope so the beds are on a flat surface.

- Consider whether one area of your yard is colder than another. One kitchen gardener we know placed her garden at the bottom of a slope and up against a fence. In the spring and fall, cold frosty air came down the slope and was trapped against the fence.
- Place your garden as close to a water supply as possible. This will save you time and trips back and forth during the gardening season.

Putting Your Garden on Paper

Begin by putting your garden plan on paper, even if it is a small garden. Some gardeners draw this plan to scale (for example, making $1/4$ inch equal 1 foot), which allows them to allocate space accurately. Others simply draw a rough sketch and go from there. I like to use graph paper because it enables me to see at a glance how much space I have. With a 5-foot bed, I let each square equal 2 inches, and with a 10-foot bed, 4 inches. Graphing allows you to easily plant in small groups. You can count the number of plants, or even seeds, that you are going to use.

Here are a few tips:

- Major vegetables such as tomatoes, peppers, and eggplants should be surrounded by secondary vegetables or herbs: green onions, bush beans, celery. Plant vegetables that mature quickly between those that mature more slowly. For instance, plant radishes in the same space in which you have transplanted tomatoes. Harvest the radishes four to five weeks before the tomato vines take over the space. You can also use this same space underneath the grown tomatoes as a microclimate for radishes in warm weather to ensure a continuous supply of radishes long after they stop growing in the regular garden.

- Plant vines (cucumbers, melons, peas, squash) against a fence or support at the north end of your garden. This ensures that the smaller plants get enough sun each day and keeps them from being shaded out by the taller plants. Use smaller vertical supports within the interior of the garden. These can be planted with bush varieties of cucumbers and winter squash.

- Include herbs and flowers in every garden. Certain plants can repel or attract insects. Borage, for instance, can attract bees, while marigolds are said to keep bean beetles away from snap beans and to repel nematodes. Garlic and chives may repel aphids. We urge you to put herbs and flowers among the vegetables when you have the space.

- Plan successive plantings of such vegetables as beans, lettuce, and radishes. This ensures a continued supply of these vegetables throughout the growing season.

- Make sure you space all major plants properly on your plan. Winter squash, for instance, requires at least 12 inches between plant centers (if grown up a fence). This means that if you have a 5-by-5-foot garden, you can plant six squash across the north end to grow up the vertical support frame. Use a compass to draw a 12-inch circle (on paper) around each plant.

Twelve Garden Plans

We offer twelve kitchen garden plans that you can use to design your own garden. Just adjust them to fit your own needs. See Figures 1-6 to 1-17.

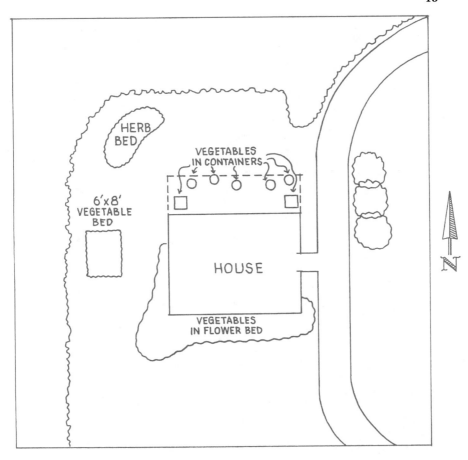

Figure 1-6. Kitchen gardens can be planted in sections rather than in one big bed.

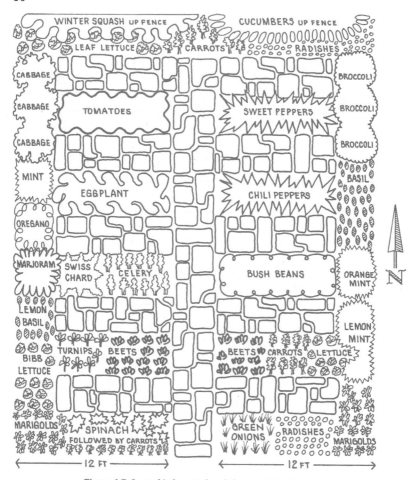

WINTER SQUASH UP FENCE   CUCUMBERS UP FENCE

LEAF LETTUCE   CARROTS   RADISHES

CABBAGE

CABBAGE   TOMATOES   SWEET PEPPERS

CABBAGE

MINT

EGGPLANT   CHILI PEPPERS

OREGANO

MARJORAM   SWISS
CHARD   CELERY   BUSH BEANS

LEMON
BASIL

BIBB
LETTUCE   TURNIPS   BEETS   BEETS   CARROTS   LETTUCE

MARIGOLDS   SPINACH
FOLLOWED BY CARROTS   GREEN
ONIONS   RADISHES   MARIGOLDS

BROCCOLI

BROCCOLI

BROCCOLI

BASIL

ORANGE
MINT

LEMON
MINT

N

|← 12 FT →| |← 12 FT →|

Figure 1-7. Large kitchen garden. Select varieties from text.

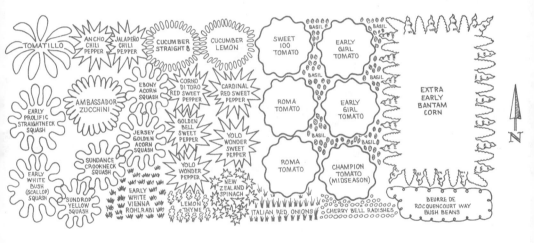

Figure 1-8. Summer kitchen garden. 10' x 4' bed.

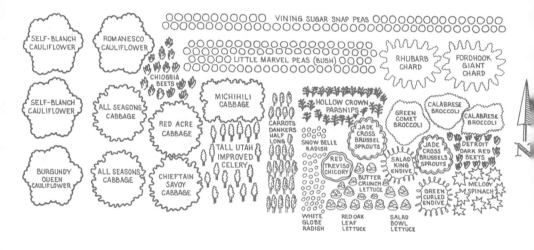

Figure 1-9. Fall/spring kitchen garden. 10' x 4' bed.

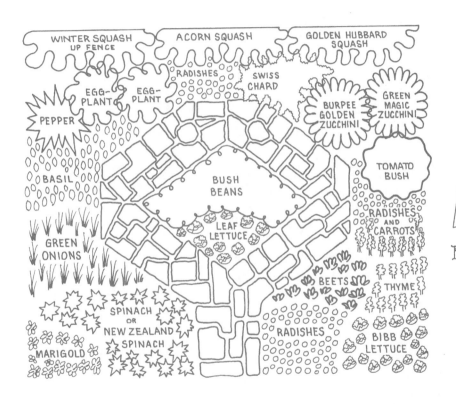

WINTER SQUASH UP FENCE

ACORN SQUASH

GOLDEN HUBBARD SQUASH

RADISHES

SWISS CHARD

EGG-PLANT

EGG-PLANT

PEPPER

BURPEE GOLDEN ZUCCHINI

GREEN MAGIC ZUCCHINI

BASIL

TOMATO BUSH

BUSH BEANS

RADISHES AND CARROTS

LEAF LETTUCE

GREEN ONIONS

BEETS

THYME

SPINACH OR NEW ZEALAND SPINACH

RADISHES

BIBB LETTUCE

MARIGOLD

N

Figure 1-10. Select varieties from text. 10' x 7' bed.

20

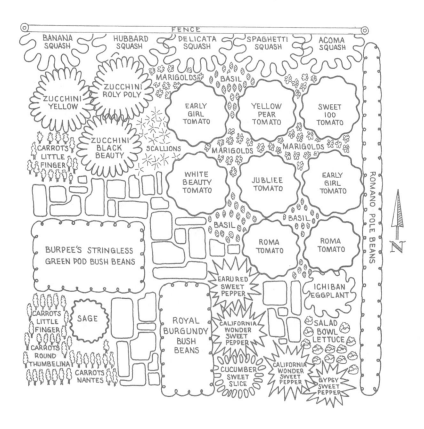

Figure 1-11. Large kitchen garden possibilities. 9' x 9' bed.

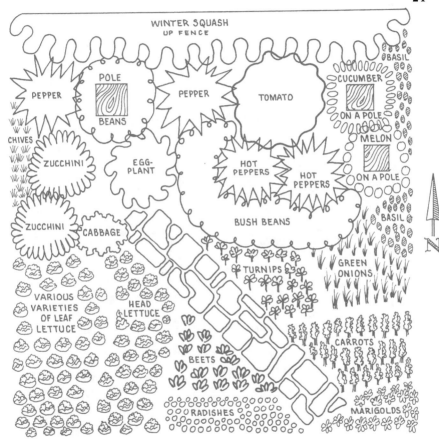

Figure 1-12. General kitchen garden. Select varieties from text. Plant and harvest peas before planting winter squash. Plant radishes at 2-week intervals. Intercrop radishes, leaf lettuce, and green onion with larger plants, and harvest before they take over the space. 5' x 5' bed.

22

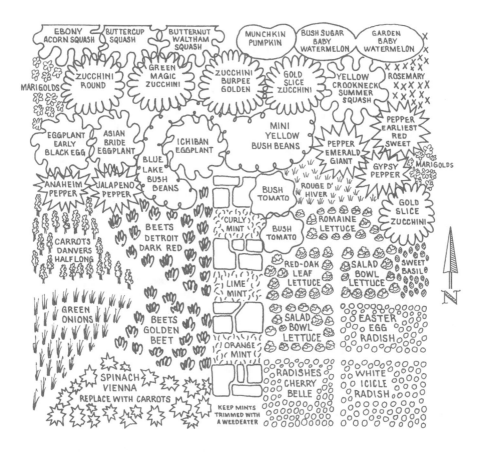

Figure 1-13. Kitchen garden stressing winter and summer varieties. 6' x 6' bed.

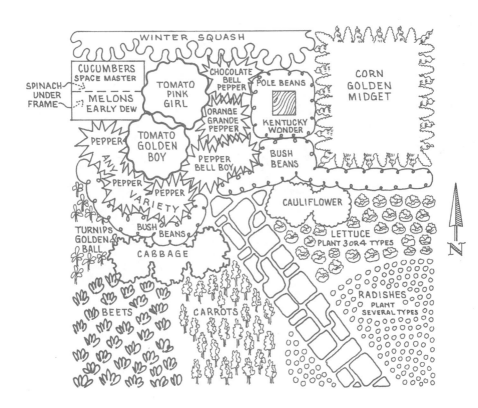

Figure 1-14. Kitchen garden. Plant peas before winter squash. Intercrop radishes, leaf lettuce, and green onion with larger plants. 4' x 4' bed.

24

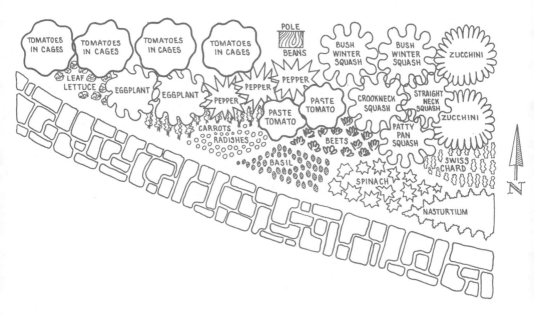

Figure 1-15. Flower bed kitchen garden.

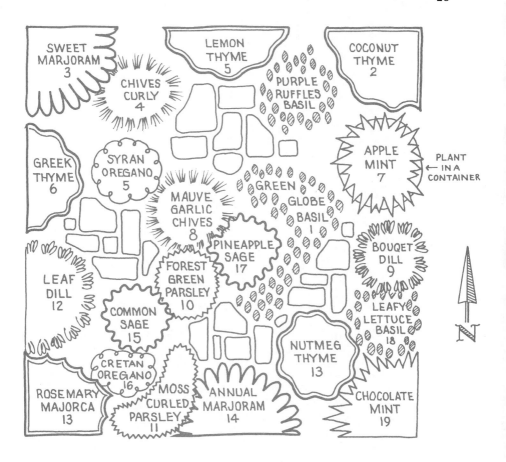

Figure 1-16. Gourmet herb garden. 4' x 4' bed.

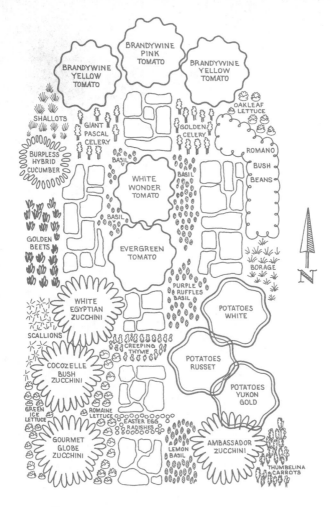

Figure 1-17. Experimental kitchen garden. 5' x 10' bed.

Chapter Two

The Intensive Gardening Method

Intensive gardening techniques can double or triple the quantities of vegetables you can grow in a given space. Intensive gardening requires that you plant vegetables all the way across the bed instead of in rows. A 5-foot-by-5-foot garden, for instance, can yield approximately two hundred tomatoes, one hundred carrots, fifty beets, all the lettuce you can eat, and more.

Creating Super Soil

Specially prepared soil is the heart of the postage stamp kitchen garden. The secret to building this soil can be expressed in five words: *add plenty of organic material.* No matter what type of soil you have, organic material will physically improve the structure of that soil.

Clay soil has limited air space, and the tiny clay particles lump together to hold the water. Spading or tilling organic material into clay soil loosens the soil by getting between the soil particles and by acting as a glue to hold the clay particles together in small crumbs. We live in the Sierra Nevada foothills, clay soil country. To create our super soil, we add about 10 inches of horse manure every year. This can be brought in from a local ranch if you live near one. We like aged horse manure to assure we won't have any weed seeds. We spread the manure about 4 inches deep, then till and add 4 more inches, then till again until thoroughly blended. With well-aged manure and double blending, there is no objectionable odor.

Sandy soils pose a different problem. The large irregular particles leave too much air space and simply won't hold water. You can water sandy soil one hour, and it will be dry the next. Dolly, a gardening friend of ours, has sandy soil, a real detriment since she lives in the Sacramento valley where the summers are hot and dry. To correct this problem, she adds fall leaves and tills in 4 inches of compost plus a couple of inches of steer manure. The organic particles fill the space and act like a sponge to hold the water.

The Bacterial Wrecking Crew

Besides improving the soil structure in all types of soil, organic material works in another way by giving the soil bacteria something to feed on. Good soil structure increases the temperature, air, and water necessary for maximum bacterial action. As soil temperature rises in the spring, bacterial action increases, breaking down the organic matter into nutrients that plants can use. To keep the soil structure in good condition, you must continually add new organic material. Most gardeners do this once a year.

Some of the best organic material are compost, peat moss, leaf mold, sawdust, animal manures, and commercial organic mixes. We'll review each type here.

Compost consists of one or more organic materials that decompose to the point where the materials break readily into elements that plants can absorb. It contains decaying materials such as leaves, manure, grass clippings, food scraps, and similar items. This is probably one of the best organic materials you can add since it also supplies some nutrients. We suggest that when you first start your kitchen garden, you should buy compost from a garden supply store, but after that you will probably want to make your own. Later in this chapter, we'll show you how to create no-fuss, no-odor compost in an outdoor bin or even in a garbage can set in the corner of a garage.

Peat moss contains the decomposed remains of prehistoric plants. This is a favorite organic conditioner of many gardeners. It retains water and nutrients well. Peat moss is acidic, however, so when you add peat moss, we suggest that you buy a simple pH kit from a nursery and check your soil pH. Most vegetables like soil that is neither acidic nor alkaline. If the test shows that your soil is too acidic, you will need to add dolomite lime (instructions appear later in this chapter).

Leaf mold makes a good organic soil additive. Leaf mold contains nitrogen, phosphorus, and potassium in sufficient quantities to support good growth. Almost any leaves will do, including maple, oak, and sycamore. Several oaks grow on our property, so we collect the leaves in the fall for composting. We build a 4-foot-high pile of leaves and add blood meal to speed up the composting process. We cover the pile with black plastic to help the leaves retain moisture. We'll discuss composting in more detail in the next section.

Sawdust is one of the best granular conditioners available. It is easy to use and long lasting. Sawdust, however, ties up the nitrogen in the soil. You will need to add about $\frac{1}{2}$ pound of pure nitrogen per 10 cubic yards of sawdust.

Animal manures are vital to your garden. They help build good soil and add many nutrients, especially nitrogen. Each, however, has different properties and varying amounts of nitrogen, phosphorus, and potassium. Chicken, horse, sheep, and rabbit manures are known as "hot" manures because of their high nitrogen content. Cow manures are "cold" manures because they are low in nitrogen and break down fairly slowly. We prefer horse manure because, even in the city, there's always a stable around. Most will gladly give the manure to you at no cost, or even deliver it for a small fee.

Commercial organic mixes are also very popular. Demand has been so great for organic soil mixes that many nurseries and landscape material firms stockpile huge quantities of this material and sell it by the cubic yard. Some contain both animal manures and mushroom compost. A 25-square-foot bed needs about $^2/_3$ cubic yard of organic material per bed. A 100-square-foot garden needs about $2^1/_2$ cubic yards of material. Most firms will deliver at no charge if you buy in large enough quantities. If your time is valuable, we suggest that you buy a commercial mix.

Creating Compost for Your Garden

Compost is simply a decayed mixture of grass clippings, leaves, and other organic materials. Good compost depends on the particle size, the amount of nitrogen available, the heat produced, the moisture in the pile, and how often the pile is turned.

The smaller the particle size, the faster the decomposition because the bacteria has more surface to work on. If the leaves, stems, and other materials are shredded before they are added to the compost pile, they will decay faster and be ready sooner. We suggest that you buy a good chipper/shredder to reduce large materials to quick composting size.

While leaves make one of the best organic conditioners, they are hard to compost because they mostly contain carbon. You can correct this by adding nitrogen in the form of blood meal, grass clippings, or chicken manure. Here are two rules to follow:

1. Compost must heat up to between 140° to 160°F for good bacterial action to occur. Small compost piles lose heat readily. A good minimum size for a "quick-cooking" compost is 3 cubic feet.
2. Every pile needs moisture for decomposition. You can keep the pile's moisture content right by making sure that it has about the same consistency as a squeezed out sponge. Watch out, since the pile can really get hot. If necessary, add water until the pile has the right consistency. Don't overdo it. Too much water can cut down on the oxygen available to the bacteria.

A compost pile must be turned every two to three days to keep the bacterial action going. You can turn the material with a small hand cultivator so the top and sides are moved to the center. This allows air penetration and also brings uncomposted materials to the center where most of the action takes place. See Table 2-1 to learn how to correct any problems.

Composting in a Can

For small gardens (25 square feet or less), composting in a garbage can is perfect. The can takes little space, is easy to handle (just pop in your materials every day), and doesn't smell. Here are the steps:

1. Start with a galvanized 30-gallon can and punch several holes in the bottom with a hammer and a large nail. Place the can on a few bricks, and put a pan underneath to catch any liquid that might drain out.

TABLE 2-1. COMPOST TROUBLESHOOTING		
SYMPTOMS	**PROBLEM**	**SOLUTION**
The compost has a bad odor	Not enough air	Turn it
The center of the pile is dry	Not enough water	Moisten materials while turning the pile
The compost is damp and warm in the middle but nowhere else	Too small	Collect more material and mix the old ingredients into a new pile
The heap is damp and sweet-smelling but still will not heat up	Lack of nitrogen	Mix in a nitrogen source such as fresh grass clippings, fresh manure, blood meal, or ammonium sulfate

2. Put a 3-inch layer of soil or peat moss at the bottom of the can.
3. Add 2 or 3 inches of kitchen scraps (excluding meat). Then add a 2-inch layer of grass clippings, shredded newspaper, and/or shredded leaves. Continue this layering until the can is full. Add these materials every few days as you collect them.
4. Place the lid on the can. The ripe compost will be ready in 3 to 4 months. If you start the can in the fall, the compost will be ready to add to your garden by spring. You don't have to worry about the moisture content, and the can doesn't have to be turned. This

container can be placed in the corner of a garden, in the garage, or in an out of the way place in the yard.

Composting in a Bin

We suggest that if your garden reaches 50 square feet or more, you should compost in a bin. You can build the bin with a dozen 1-inch-by-12-inch boards, each 30 inches long. Nail four boards together to make a frame, or bottomless box, and place this on the site. Use the remaining boards to make two more frames, and stack these to complete the bin.

Build your compost in layers. Put down a 6-inch layer of plant refuse, grass clippings, kitchen scraps, and leaves. Add a 2-inch layer of good garden soil. Repeat this procedure until the pile reaches the top of the bin. Then add a 1-inch soil cover. We also recommend two types of commercial composters. The Backyard Composter is a plastic bin composed of recycled materials designed to trap solar heat. It has adjustable air vents and a sliding bottom door. The Nova Wood compost bin is built from recycled plastic slats that look like gray, weathered cedar. The front has removable slats so that it is easy to harvest your compost. These are ideal for kitchen gardeners who are fussy about the appearance of their gardens.

Plants Get Hungry Too

Despite the fact that nutrition is just as important to plants as it is to people, many gardeners ignore the problem. Then they wonder what's wrong with their vegetables. Vegetables generally need fifteen nutrients for good growth. Three elements—oxygen, carbon, and hydrogen—come from air and water. The other twelve exist in the soil. Nitrogen, phosphorus, and potassium are the major macronutrients needed by vegetables in large amounts.

Magnesium, manganese, copper, zinc, iron, sulfur, calcium, molybdenum, and boron are secondary or micronutrients and are needed in very small quantities. Let's take a close look at the major elements and see what they do for vegetables.

Nitrogen is the green giant that your plants need for lush growth. It's the element that produces leaf growth and vigorous dark green leaves. It helps produce plant proteins and a healthy root system, increases the set of fruit, and helps feed soil micro-organisms. It is the nutrient most familiar to gardeners and is especially important for such leafy vegetables such as cabbage, lettuce, spinach, and collards. Nitrogen deficiency causes leaves to lose their healthy green color and turn yellow. This yellowing usually begins at the base of the plant and works its way up the leaves.

Excess nitrogen delays flowering, produces excessive leaf growth, reduces the quality of the fruits, and renders crops less resistant to disease. Aphid infestation is another symptom. Tomatoes with too much nitrogen, for instance, will be almost all vine and no fruit.

There are a number of natural sources of nitrogen. These include blood meal, bone meal, and fish scraps. See Table 2-2, and select one source for your garden.

TABLE 2-2. MAJOR NATURAL SOURCES OF NITROGEN

MATERIAL	NITROGEN (PERCENT)	APPLY PER 100 SQUARE FEET
Blood meal	15.0	5–10 pounds
Cottonseed meal	8.0	10 pounds
Fish meal	8.0	5–10 pounds
Bat guano	10.0	5 pounds

Phosphorus. All growing plants need phosphorus, which stimulates early root formation, hastens maturity, and is important for fruit, flower, and seed development. It also helps provide disease resistance. Phosphorus deficiency causes dark or bluish green leaves followed by bronzing, red-dening, or purpling, especially along veins and margins. Lower leaves are sometimes yellow, drying to greenish brown or black. Plants are often stunted and spindly and mature late. Watch for purple leaves, veins, and stems. Radish leaves develop a reddish tint on the undersides. Leaves of corn turn yellow at blossoming time. Excess phosphorus produces iron and zinc deficiencies in corn, beans, tomatoes, and other plants.

Natural sources of phosphorous include phosphate rock and steamed bone meal. Choose a source from Table 2-3.

TABLE 2-3. MAJOR NATURAL SOURCES OF PHOSPHORUS		
MATERIAL	**PHOSPHORUS (PERCENT)**	**APPLY PER 100 SQUARE FEET**
Phosphate rock	16.0	5 pounds
Bone meal, steamed	11.0	5 pounds

Potassium (potash) is important in the manufacture of sugar and starches. It increases photosynthesis. It improves the color of flowers and the length of time the fruit is edible. Potash promotes vigorous root systems and is essential in growing good root crops. It produces strong stems and reduces water loss by helping the openings of the leaf pores (stomata) to close tight-ly when water is in short supply. It increases vigor, helps fight disease, and reduces winter kill.

Potash deficiency causes the edges of the leaves to turn brown and curl. There may be small dead areas along the margins and between the leaf veins. Curled carrot leaves indicate a potash deficiency. Excess potash produces coarse, poorly colored fruit.

Natural sources include wood ash and green sand. Choose a source from Table 2-4.

TABLE 2-4. MAJOR NATURAL SOURCES OF POTASH		
MATERIAL	POTASH (PERCENT)	APPLY PER 100 SQUARE FEET
Wood ashes	8.0	5 pounds
Green sand	7.0	5 pounds
Granite dust	5.0	5 pounds

Playing Doctor with Your Soil

There are a number of ways you can determine how fertile your soil is. First, plants will let you know by their appearance (see Table 2-5). Still, these symptoms aren't specific enough to allow you to correct the problem because some symptoms show up in several different nutrient deficiencies. They're a first alert. Before you can cure a problem, you must determine exactly what the problem is.

In most states, you can take soil samples and have them tested free or for a small fee through the State Cooperative Extension Service agent in your county. Commercial soil laboratories will also test your soil for a fee. You'll find these listed in the telephone yellow pages under "Laboratories, testing soil."

TABLE 2-5. SOIL NUTRIENT DEFICIENCY

SYMPTOM	CAUSE	NUTRIENT SOLUTION
Yellow leaves starting with the lower leaves; stunted growth	Nitrogen deficiency	Apply blood meal at the rate of 10 ounces per 100 square feet
Bluish green leaves followed by bronzing or purpling, drying to a greenish-brown or black	Phosphorus deficiency	Apply phosphate rock at the rate of $3/4$ pound per 100 square feet, or test soil and follow recommendations
Dry or scorched leaves; dead areas along margins; plants stunted; rusty appearance	Potash (potassium) deficiency	Apply wood ashes or greensand at the rate of $1^1/_4$–$1^1/_2$ pounds per 100 square feet, or test soil and follow recommendations
Mottling of lower leaves at margins or tips or between veins; leaves wilt from bottom up	Magnesium deficiency	Use 1 pound of Epsom salt per 1000 square feet, or test soil and follow recommendations
Mottled yellowing leaves; stunted growth	Manganese deficiency	Use manganese sulfate, or test soil and follow recommendations
Dark green, olive gray leaf edges; edges curl upward	Copper deficiency	Use 6 ounces of copper sulfate per 1000 square feet, or test soil and follow recommendations

(continued on next page)

TABLE 2-5. SOIL NUTRIENT DEFICIENCY (CONTINUED)		
SYMPTOM	CAUSE	NUTRIENT SOLUTION
Mottling, yellowing, or scorching of the tissues between veins	Zinc deficiency	Use 8 ounces of zinc sulfate per 1000 square feet, or test soil and follow recommendations
Yellow leaves; green veins	Iron deficiency	Use a soluble iron complex, iron sulfate, or chelated iron, or test soil and follow recommendations
Young leaves turn pale green to yellow; older leaves remain green	Sulfur deficiency	Most soils contain adequate amounts of sulfur; if not, test soil and follow recommendations
Stem tips die; distortion of young stems	Calcium deficiency	Spray plants with calcium nitrate or add calcium sulfate (gypsum), or test soil and follow recommendations
Leaves turn pale green or yellow; leaves crinkled, stunted	Molybdenum deficiency	Use about 1 teaspoon of sodium or ammonium molybdate per 1000 square feet, or test soil and follow recommendations

You can also purchase soil test kits through a nursery or a mail order firm. When you take a soil sample, select soil from eight to fifteen zigzag spots throughout the garden instead of taking all the soil from one spot.

Most tests generally state whether your soil is deficient in nitrogen (N), phosphorus (P), and/or potash (potassium) (K). Typically the results include specific fertilizer recommendations. Most labs will not usually test for secondary or minor elements. Table 2-6 shows the composition of many natural plant foods.

Most do-it-yourself kits test for nitrogen, phosphorus, and potassium. One popular kit uses a color chart that rates the severity of the nitrogen, phosphorus, and potassium deficiency. You simply match the color of the

TABLE 2-6. NATURAL PLANT FOODS				
TYPE	**SOURCE**	**COMPOSITION (%)**		
		N	P	K
Animal manures	Cattle	0.53	0.29	0.48
(fresh)	Chicken	0.89	0.48	0.83
	Horse	0.55	0.27	0.57
	Sheep	0.89	0.48	0.83
Animal manures	Cattle	2.00	1.80	3.00
(dried)	Horse	0.80	0.20	0.60
	Sheep	1.40	1.00	3.00
Organic nutrients	Dried blood meal	9–14	-	-
	Bone meal	1.6–2.5	23–25	-
	Fish emulsion	5–10	2.0	2.0
Pulverized rock	Rock phosphate	-	38–41	-
powders	Greensand	-	1.35	4.1–9.5
Vegetable	Cottonseed meal	6.7–7.4	2–3	1.5–2.0
	Seaweed	1.7	0.8	5.0
	Soybean meal	6.0	1.0	2.0
	Oak leaves	0.8	0.4	0.2
	Wood ashes	-	1.5	7.0

test sample in the tube to the color on the chart. The chart rates the severity of the deficiency, and the instructions tell you how much nitrogen, phosphorus, and potassium you need to add.

You can buy organic nutrient mixes already formulated from commercial sources. We buy ours in 50-pound sacks. You can find complete organic fertilizers at most nurseries and garden centers. For every 25 square feet of garden, add 3 quarts of these mixes.

If you like, you can always make your own nutrient mix. Mix 1 quart of blood meal and 2 quarts of bone meal with either 1 quart of greensand or 1 quart of wood ash. We suggest that you make this up and store it in gallon bottles, such as empty plastic milk bottles.

Acid or Alkaline?

Tell gardeners that their soil is too acid or too alkaline, and they will nod knowingly. Tell them that their soil has a pH of 5.7, and as often as not, they will give you a blank stare. Soil scientists express acid (sour soil) or alkaline (sweet soil) in terms of pH on a scale of 1 to 14. It's actually pretty simple: 7 is neutral; below 7 is acid; above 7 is alkaline.

Vegetables, however, are as finicky as people. Each type has its own particular pH requirements (see Table 2-7). Potatoes, for instance, do fine in a fairly acid soil (pH range of 4.8 to 6.3). Tomatoes straddle the fence, growing well in acid to slightly alkaline soil (pH range of 5 to 7.5). Beets and cabbage dip their toes into both the acid and alkaline range (pH range of 6 to 8). Since it's impractical to make one section of your garden one pH and another a different pH, most gardeners compromise on a slightly acid to neutral soil (pH 6.5 to 7).

If your soil is too alkaline, your plants will sometimes show yellow leaves, stunted growth, and burned leaf margins. Alkaline soils can some-

TABLE 2-7. OPTIMUM pH RANGE FOR VEGETABLES	
pH	**VEGETABLE**
6 to 8	Beets, cabbage, melons
6 to 7.5	Peas, spinach, summer squash
6 to 7	Cauliflower, celery, chives, endive, horseradish, lettuce, onions, radishes, rhubarb
5.5 to 7.5	Corn, pumpkins, tomatoes
5.5 to 6.8	Beans, carrots, cucumbers, parsnips, peppers, rutabaga, winter squash
5.5 to 6.5	Eggplant, watermelon
4.8 to 6.3	Potatoes

times be too salty. Acid soils are not easy to detect visually and will generally require a pH test.

Testing for pH

For a number of years, we got by quite well without testing the soil. We determined by trial and error what grew well in our soil and what didn't. Then we discovered that testing the pH is easy and that it made a difference in how our crops grew. The easiest device to use is a soil test tape. To find the pH of your garden, just press the tape against the soil and compare the color of the tape to the colors on a pH chart. A pH kit works on the same principle, but uses liquid instead of a tape. A pH meter works electrically. When its prongs are placed in the soil, the pH is automatically registered on the scale.

To counteract *acid soil*, add ground dolomite lime at the rate of about 4 pounds per 100 square feet for each unit of pH below 6.5. To correct *alkaline soil*, add sulfur at the rate of about 4 pounds per 100 square feet for each unit of pH above 7. Follow the directions on the package.

Getting Your Soil Ready

Here's what we recommend. Lay out your bed of any size, and then place a 5- to 6-inch layer of organic material on top of it. Run a rototiller over the bed several times. If your bed is more than 25 square feet, cultivate with a conventional rototiller. For beds less than 25 square feet, we recommend a minitiller.

When you're finished rototilling, take a spading fork and loosen the soil as far below the cultivated soil as possible. Then rake the rototilled bed and add either commercial organic nutrients or your own mix. Use 3 quarts of nutrients for every 25 square feet of garden bed. For 4-by-4-foot beds, apply slightly less than 2 quarts of nutrient.

If you don't mind the work, you can also create small beds by hand. Sprinkle 3 quarts of nutrient for every 25 square feet of bed, and then spread 6 to 8 inches of organic material over the top of the bed. Dig a trench along one side, one spade deep. Put the topsoil outside the bed. Loosen the soil in the trench 8 to 10 inches deep. Dig a second trench beside the first one. Fill the first trench with the soil from the second. Again loosen the soil in the empty trench 8 to 10 inches. Repeat across the bed, and use the soil from the prior trench to fill the next. Rake the top of the bed and plant. See figure 2-1a–c.

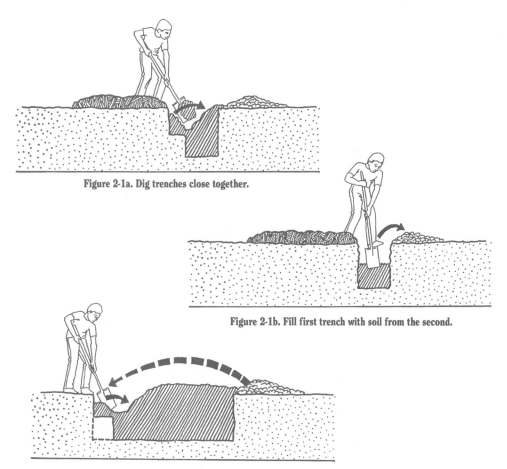

Figure 2-1a. Dig trenches close together.

Figure 2-1b. Fill first trench with soil from the second.

Figure 2-1c. Repeat process across the trench.

Figure 2-2. Wood frame boxes

Raised beds also make good kitchen gardens (Figure 2-2). You can make permanent boxes out of timber, stone, bricks, or blocks, or you can use a plastic raised bed kit. You can construct these beds a few inches high or high enough to let you sit on the edge.

A lot of kitchen gardeners place one or two 4-by-4-foot beds near their back door. The simplest way to construct them is to nail (or screw) together redwood, cedar, or pressure-treated 2-by-12-inch boards directly in place. Reinforce the corners with 2-by-2 inch posts. Extend the posts about 12 inches into the ground to anchor the box in place. You can top this with a 2-by-6-inch cap as a seat. Most gardeners fill these raised beds with a commercial soil preparation.

Whichever method you use, you will have a super soil that will allow you to grow large quantities of vegetables across your beds.

Planting for Success

Planting for success means growing the largest quantity of vegetables throughout the entire growing season. Select warm-season crops such as tomatoes and peppers for summer planting. Then select cool-season crops

TABLE 2-8. VEGETABLES BY GROWING SEASON

SPRING	SUMMER	FALL
Beets	Beans	Beets
Broccoli	Cucumbers	Broccoli
Brussels Sprouts	Corn	Carrots
Carrots	Eggplant	Kohlrabi
Cabbage	Melons	Lettuce
Cauliflower	Peppers	Radishes
Onions	Pumpkins	Spinach
Radishes	Squash	Turnip
Scallions	Tomatoes	
Turnip		

TABLE 2-9. WARM- AND COOL-SEASON CROPS

COOL SEASON*	WARM SEASON**	INTOLERANT OF FROST AT MATURITY
Asparagus	Beans	Carrots
Beets	Corn	Cauliflower
Broccoli	Cucumbers	Endive
Brussels Sprouts	Eggplant	Lettuce
Cabbage	Melons	Peas
Kale	Okra	Rhubarb
Mustard greens	Peppers	Swiss Chard
Onions	Squash	
Radishes	Tomatoes	
Spinach		
Spinach, New Zealand		
Turnip		
Rutabaga		

*Adapted to 55°–70°F. Will tolerate some frost.
**Require 65°–80°F day and night. Readily damaged by frost.

such as cabbage and spinach for spring and fall planting. See Tables 2-8 and 2-9.

Small square beds should be planted with the large vegetables at the north end. Plant root and leafy vegetables facing the south end of the garden. Here are the specifics:

1. Plant vegetables such as peas, winter squash, melons, and cucumbers at the north end of the bed up a fence or trellis in a zone about 1 foot wide. Start these plants from seed directly in the garden. Space them according to the directions on the seed package, or as described in Table 2-10.

2. In the middle part of a small bed (in a 2- to 3-foot zone), grow tomatoes, pole beans (around a single pole), broccoli, cabbage, cauliflower, eggplant, peppers, summer squash, and bush varieties of melons and winter squash. Buy broccoli, cabbage, cauliflower, eggplant, peppers, and tomatoes as plants, and transplant them into your garden. Start special varieties inside before you intend to set them out in the garden (see Table 2-11). We will discuss starting plants from seed later in this chapter.

3. In the lower third of the bed, plant the root and leafy plants: beets, lettuce, carrots, and so on. Sow these seeds across the allotted space for each vegetable. To get the right spacing, you might want to practice with coffee grounds first; they won't harm your garden.

If you are planting in long, narrow beds that run from west to east, plant the larger crops up supports at the east end of the beds. Grow tomatoes, pole beans, eggplant, peppers, and similar-sized vegetables in the middle section of the bed. In the westerly third, grow the root and leafy

TABLE 2-10. INTENSIVE PLANT SPACING IN INCHES

VEGETABLE	SPACING	VEGETABLE	SPACING
Asparagus	12	Leeks	3
Bean, fava	4	Lettuce, head	10
Bean, lima (pole)	10	Lettuce, leaf	6
Bean, lima (bush)	8	Muskmelon	12
Bean, snap (pole)	6	Okra	16
Bean, snap (bush)	4	Onions, bunching	2
Beets	3	Onions	3–4
Broccoli	15	Parsnip	4
Brussels sprouts	15	Peas	2-3
Cabbage, Chinese	10	Peppers	12–24
Cabbage	14	Potatoes	4–10
Carrot	2	Pumpkins	12–18
Cauliflower	15	Radishes	2
Celeriac	8	Rutabaga	6
Celery	6	Shallot	2
Collards	12	Spinach, New Zealand	10
Corn	8	Spinach	4
Cucumbers	6	Squash, summer	12
Eggplant	24	Squash, winter	12–24
Garlic	3	Swiss chard	6
Horseradish	6	Tomatoes	18
Kale	8	Turnip	3
Kohlrabi	6	Watermelon	12–18

TABLE 2-11. WHEN TO START SEEDLINGS INDOORS

1 MONTH*	2 MONTHS*	3 MONTHS*
Celeriac	Broccoli	Brussels Sprouts
Eggplant	Cabbage	Lettuce
Leeks	Cauliflower	Pumpkins
Onions	Melons	Squash
Peppers	Tomatoes	

*Before you intend to plant in garden

vegetables such as beets, carrots, spinach, and turnips. This arrangement allows you to garden vertically in the east end of a long bed without shading the smaller plants.

If you are planting in three or more long narrow beds, plant the tall vegetables in the north bed, the middle-sized vegetables in the middle bed, and the leafy and root vegetables in the southern beds.

Starting Plants from Seed

The easiest way to start a kitchen garden is to buy some of the plants from a nursery as seedlings. However, if you want to grow quantities of special varieties as described in this book, you will need to order these varieties from a catalog seed firm and grow them from seed. See the Appendix for a list of suppliers.

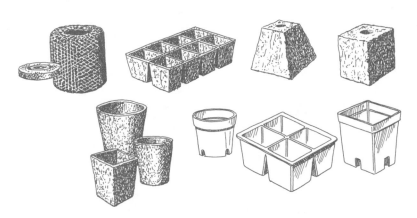

Figure 2-3. Containers for starting seeds using the one-step method.

There are two methods for starting seedlings in a west- or south-facing window, the one-step method and the two-step method.

The One-Step Method

With the one-stepmethod, you can sow seeds directly in a small pot or cube made of biodegradable material. When seedlings reach transplant size, they are placed in the garden, pots and all (Figure 2-4). The roots will then grow through the pot walls and spread into the surrounding soil.

Several kinds of containers for transplanting are shown in Figure 2-3. You can select from Jiffy 7-type pellets (compressed sterile sphagnum peat held in place by a net or binder), peat pots, or cell pots.

Figure 2-4. One-step method for starting seeds.

Here's how to grow vegetables and flowers using the one-step method:

1. Choose any of the containers shown in Figure 2-3. Fill the biodegradable pots with a commercial planting mix purchased from a garden center or nursery.
2. Dampen the biodegradable pots in water, and soak them until they expand.
3. Sow the seeds directly into the pots.
4. Place the pots on a tray, and put the tray and the containers inside a plastic bag. Blow up the bag like a balloon, and secure the end with a wire tie.
5. Keep the bag at room temperature, in a window, out of direct light. Keep the containers damp but not soaked.
6. When the plants are 7 inches tall, they are ready to be hardened off and planted in your garden. Hardening off means gradually adapting an indoor-grown seedling to outdoor weather.

You can also buy window greenhouses from your garden center or seed catalogs that make growing seedlings a snap.

The Two-Step Method

With the "Two-Step Method" (Figure 2-5), you sow a number of seeds in a container and when the seedlings are large enough, move them to individual pots. These plants are then transplanted into the garden at a later date.

Use this method when you intend to grow large quantities of small vegetables such as onions or lettuce. It is also suited to growing cabbage and cauliflower. Do not start beans, cucumbers, melons, peas, pumpkins, and squash together in large containers because their root systems cannot take the shock of being transplanted into the garden. Use the one-step method for those vegetables. Here are the directions for step one of the two-step method:

1. Fill the container with planting mix and level it off with a knife. Then lightly press down and wet the mix thoroughly before planting seeds.
2. Scatter small seeds such as lettuce over the entire container. Cover with about $^1/_4$ inch of mix.
3. Sow large- or medium-sized seeds in furrows made with a pencil. Space large seeds 1 inch apart and medium-sized seeds 2 inches apart. When you finish planting, water lightly.
4. To achieve the proper humidity, seal the trays in a clear plastic bag, and set them on a bright windowsill out of the sunlight.
5. Don't water again until after germination (when the little sprouts poke through the soil). After that, add only enough water to keep the soil mix damp. Check the soil moisture with your fingers.
6. When seedlings are 1 or 2 inches high, thin so they stand about 2 inches apart. Keep the healthy, vigorous

Figure 2-5. Step one: Begin seeds in a small container.

seedlings, and remove the small, leggy or weak ones and those that look like they might be diseased. To avoid damaging the entangled roots of nearby plants, don't yank the seedlings; clip them with small scissors.

7. When the seedlings are 3 or 4 inches tall, remove them from the bag and allow them to grow in a south-facing window.

Here are the directions for step two:

1. When the first true leaves have formed, "prick" out the seedlings with a spoon, and gently lift them from the soil. The first two leaflike appendages are not true leaves; they're cotyledons, or "seed leaves." Don't prick until you see the third and succeeding leaves appear.

2. Prepare an individual container for each seedling. Dig a small hole in the planting mix, spread the seedling's roots, and gently push the soil around the roots. Vegetables with a long taproot (such as eggplant, peppers, and tomatoes) should be planted fairly deep. The roots will grow from the buried part of the stem. Plant broccoli, cabbage, cauliflower, and lettuce so that the base of the

Figure 2-5. Step two: Transfer seedlings into individual pots.

plant is not buried. If you bury the tips, new growth will be slowed.

3. Place the newly planted containers on a tray. Insert the tray in a plastic bag, and keep the bag in dim light for a day or two. Then transfer the bag to a bright spot on a windowsill, but not in direct sunlight. Remove the seedlings from the bag as soon as they become well established.

Growing Seedlings under Lights

You can also grow seedlings indoors—under fluorescent lights—in the corner of a garage, basement, living room, kitchen, or closet. You will need at least one fluorescent fixture with two fluorescent bulbs that are marked "grow light."

Water: The Hazardous Necessity

Vegetables need adequate amounts of water to grow quickly to maturity, but give them too much or too little and you create problems. Tomato blossoms drop when they are given too much or too little water; bean pods shrivel and produce only a few seeds when they don't have enough water. Beets become stringy, radishes pithy, and carrots stumpy. With an uneven water supply lettuce becomes bitter.

While it seems complicated, there is a rule of thumb that allows you to give a kitchen garden just the right amount of water each day. Water deeply, at least two hours at a time, and then don't water again until the bed dries out to a depth of 4 to 8 inches. Check this with a trowel or a moisture sensor (a small meter that measures the moisture content of the soil).

You can water your garden by hand, water overhead, or use a drip system. Here are some basics for each.

Hand Watering

This method uses less water than overhead watering. You will find a hand wand effective for reaching underneath the leaves. This is especially useful in a small kitchen garden. Hand wands come with special seedling nozzles that produce a fine mist for newly planted seed beds and with soft rain nozzles for general purposes.

Here also are some imaginative water-stretching techniques. You can drive a plastic pipe 2 inches in diameter and 18 inches long into the ground near the base of eggplant, peppers, tomatoes, and other large vegetable plants. Pour water directly into the pipe. You can also sink large clay or plastic flower pots into the soil within 2 to 5 inches of larger plants. If possible, fill the pot with water several times a day during hot weather.

Overhead Watering

You can easily water a small kitchen garden bed using a small rotating sprinkler, a pulse sprinkler, or a stationary sprinkler with holes in the top. Most efficient are the minisprinklers that plug into a hose or drip line and deliver a spray 4 to 20 feet.

After the leaves overlap, it becomes more difficult to water thoroughly the ground of a mature garden. Some gardeners feel that overhead watering increases the danger of disease spreading throughout the garden. You can help prevent problems by watering in the morning to allow the leaves to dry out fairly quickly.

Drip Systems

A drip watering system supplies water in small amounts to the plants at ground level. Drip systems can cut water use by 50 percent. Plants generally grow better since they don't get too much or too little water. A drip system has three main parts: (1) the controls; (2) a $1/2$-inch polyethylene hose that runs throughout the garden; and (3) emitters and smaller tubing that plug into the main line to bring water directly to individual plants (Figure 2-6). We consider this the best way to water and would never be

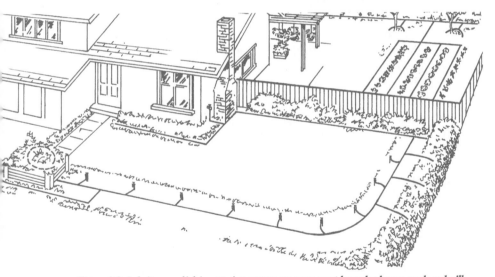

Figure 2-6. A do-it-yourself drip watering system can serve most home landscape needs and will use 40 to 60 percent less water than conventional methods. A drip system can be connected to a faucet, as shown here, or to a valve on an automatic underground sprinkler system.

without one. Our own system also uses an ooze hose and a $1/2$-inch perforated plastic line that delivers water along its length.

The controls consist of a shutoff valve (manual or electric), a filter to catch sand and foreign material, and a pressure regulator that keeps your drip system from getting too much pressure. We also use an automatic timer that turns the system off and on at the same time each day. Our timer can be set to run several layouts at the same time. This takes the guesswork out of when to water and allows us to leave for several days at a time, confident that the garden will be watered while we are gone.

If you have laid out your garden on paper, start there. Lay out your main line so that it runs throughout your bed or beds. If you have several small beds close to each other, you can run one line to all of the beds; simply bury it in between the beds. For widely spaced plants such as squash, eggplant, and tomatoes, you will want at least one, 1-gallon-per-minute emitter at each plant. For root and leaf crops that are close together, use an ooze hose or a perforated plastic hose that will run water across the entire space. You can buy drip kits and all of the other supplies at any garden supply store.

A Few More Words about Seeds

This section contains additional secrets for growing plants from seeds.

No-Spill Seed

If you are sick of seeds spilling out of your pocket while you're bent over planting, use a clothespin to hold the packet closed. Simply fold over the envelope and clip the edge. The leftover seeds will stay put.

Vegetable Seed Life

Just how many years can you keep seed until it goes bad? Garlic, okra, onion, parsnip, salsify, and shallot seeds are viable for 1 year. Leek, pepper, and rhubarb seeds keep for 2 years. Asparagus, broccoli, carrot, celery, collard, corn, kohlrabi, pea, and spinach seeds last 3 years. Bean seeds last from 3 to 5 years. Beet, Brussels sprout, cabbage, cauliflower, chard, cucumber, eggplant, kale, radish, rutabaga, squash, and tomato seeds keep for 4 years. Melon seeds last 5 years. Lettuce seeds last 6 years. See Table 2-12.

Testing Stored Seeds

To find out if your stored seed is still good, give your seed the towel test. Count out 10 seeds of the same variety on a damp paper towel. Wrap the paper towel in a wet terry cloth hand towel, and place this in a plastic bag. In six days, unwrap the seeds and count the number that have sprouted. If your germination rate is 50 percent or less, your seeds have flunked the test. Throw them on the compost heap, and order fresh seed.

Moisture Ranges for Germination

Some seeds like wet soil for germination; others like it semidry. Vegetables that germinate over the full moisture range include cabbage, carrots, cucumbers, muskmelon, onions, peppers, radishes, squash, sweet corn, tomatoes, turnip, and watermelon.

Vegetables that germinate best in moister soil include beets, endive, lettuce, lima beans, peas, and snap beans. Celery germinates only when the soil moisture is near saturation. Vegetables that germinate best in dryer soil include spinach and New Zealand spinach.

TABLE 2-12. SEED GERMINATION

VEGETABLE	MINIMUM FEDERAL STANDARD GERMINATION (%)	SEEDS PER OUNCE (AVERAGE)	RELATIVE LONGEVITY (YEARS)
Asparagus	60	1,400	3
Bean, Lima	70	20–70	3
Bean, Snap	75	100	3
Beets	65	2,000	4
Broccoli	75	8,100	3
Brussels Sprouts	70	8,500	4
Cabbage	75	7,700	4
Cabbage, Chinese	75	7,000	3
Carrots	55	22,000	3
Cauliflower	75	8,600	4
Celeriac	55	50,000	3
Celery	55	76,000	3
Chicory	65	20,000	4
Corn	75	140	2
Cucumbers	80	1,100	5
Eggplant	60	7,000	4
Endive	70	17,000	5
Kale	75	10,000	4
Kohlrabi	75	9,200	3
Leeks	60	9,900	2
Lettuce	80	26,000	6
Muskmelon	75	1,100	5
Okra	50	500	2
Onions	70	8,500	1
Parsnip	60	18,000	1
Peas	80	50–230	3
Peppers	55	4,500	2
Pumpkins	75	200	4
Radishes	75	3,100	4
Rutabaga	75	11,000	4
Salsify	75	2,000	1
Spinach	60	2,900	3
Spinach, New Zealand	40	430	3
Squash	75	180–380	4
Swiss Chard	65	1,500	4
Tomatoes	75	10,000	4
Turnip	80	14,000	4
Watermelon	70	320	4

Working Up a Lather

To sprout parsley, parsnip, and beets, scrub the seeds in a pint of warm water. If the water is hard, add $1/2$ cup of vinegar. Lather your hands with mild bath soap (not detergent), rub the seeds in your hands, and rinse them in clean water. Then soak the seeds overnight. The next day, drain the seeds on a towel and plant them. Don't let the seeds dry out during this time.

Preventing Seeds from Sinking

If spring rains sometimes sink your tiny seeds too deep into the soil to germinate and you frequently wind up with crop failure, just unroll inexpensive paper toweling in the planting rows. Scatter the seeds on top of the paper, and cover lightly with soil. The toweling keeps the seeds at the right depth while it slowly deteriorates. This way, all the seeds come up.

Seed Depth

Want a quick rule of thumb for seed depth? Plant at a depth 4 times the diameter of the seed. In wet weather or heavy soils, plant a little shallower; in light or sandy soils, plant a bit deeper.

Presprouting Magic

In a paper bag, add a cup of moist, shredded sphagnum moss. Add a pinch of seeds, and shake to mix. Roll dry material in a towel, moisten it, and wring it out. Let it stand for an hour. Twist and fold over the top of the bag, and seal it with tape or a rubber band. Place the bag in a warm place. Plant the sprouts when about half of the seeds have pushed out roots or shoots. Don't worry about the sprouts being upside down or sideways in a furrow; they will twist and turn to orient themselves.

Plant Without Bending Over

If you can't bend over to plant seeds, buy a golf club shaft protector. This plastic tube is about 3 feet long and costs about 25 cents. Place one end of the tube on the ground in the row, and then drop the seeds down the other end. You can space your seed evenly without bending over.

Seedling Problems

If you have trouble with damping off (the death of small seedlings from disease) when you start seeds in pots or flats, try planting them first in vermiculite. Just sow the seeds $^1/_4$- to $^1/_2$-inch deep in moistened vermiculite. Pat the vermiculite firm, water lightly, and slip the pot or flat into a plastic bag when the first true leaves form. Then transplant to pots or peat pots. This will give you almost 100 percent success.

Speeding Germination

Heating devices speed up germination and make seed flats comfortable for seedlings. You can buy many types, including soil warming mats, heating cables, and heated seed flats. The most elaborate are plastic tabletop greenhouses equipped with soil heater cables. This method sometimes cuts germination time in half. Studies at the University of California show that radish seeds take an average of 29 days to germinate at 41°F, but just 3 days at 86°F. Carrots germinate in an average of 50 days at 41°F, only 6 days at 86°F.

Preventing Transplant Shock

There are a number of tricks that alleviate the shock of moving transplants so that they suffer little setback or delay in growth. Follow these steps:

1. Start with small seedlings. Four to six leaves are enough.
2. Transplant at sundown or on a cloudy day.

3. Wet the soil thoroughly around the roots of seedlings a few hours before planting so that the plants will be plump with water.
4. Dig the transplanting holes before you uproot any seedlings. Fill the holes with water, and let it soak in.
5. Move the seedlings with as much soil around the roots as possible.
6. Move one plant at a time. Transplant quickly; don't delay.
7. Immediately soak the soil around each transplant. Don't wait until you have completed the row. Sprinkle the transplants daily.

Transplanting experts often move little clumps of plants at a time so as not to damage the roots by pulling individual plants apart. After the clumps have taken, thin out the excess.

You can also try cutting the potting soil around the seedlings into squares. This severs the roots that would be broken in transplanting. Since they have started to recover before you set them out, they hit the garden already growing at full speed.

Quick Seedling Protection

For protecting seedlings against frost, almost anything will do. Homemade paper hot caps, clear plastic cake covers, half a milk carton, cardboard folded over the seedlings, a cardboard box with both ends cut out and covered with clear polyethylene . . . just use your imagination.

Chapter Three

Container Gardening

By planting vegetables in containers, you can grow your kitchen garden almost anywhere, indoors or out. Start by looking for places you might squeeze in a container or two.

For patios and balcony gardens, measure your space. A 9-by-15-foot balcony, for instance, contains 135 square feet. Estimate how much space you'll need for general living, lounging, barbecuing, and so on. Then subtract this amount from the total space available. If you feel you need about half the total space for general living, you still have more than 65 square feet left in which to cultivate your kitchen garden.

Now walk through your house looking for unused space where you might grow vegetables, either in a window space or under lights. Consider bedrooms, living rooms, closets, bathrooms, and any additional interior space. You can grow many vegetables under lights—the only limit is your imagination.

You can plant in standard containers that you buy from a garden center, or you can turn almost anything into a vegetable container—the sources are endless (see Figure 3-1).

We like to shop the import stores looking for unusual baskets, which Karen turns into attractive vegetable planters. The secret is to coat the inside of the basket or box with polyester resin and strips of newspaper. First, buy clear polyester resin, hardener, and a paint brush from any craft store. Next, tear the newspaper into long strips, 5 inches wide. Brush the polyester resin on the inside of the basket's bottom and sides, and then cover the resin with newspaper strips. Continue the resin/paper process until you've lined the basket with six coats of paper. When you are finished, add an additional coat of resin.

As a general rule, the larger and deeper the container, the better the yields. While you can grow small bush-type tomatoes in smaller containers, the larger varieties require up to 20 gallons (3 cubic feet) of soil to produce a good crop.

Windowsill and Window Box Gardens

With 12 feet of sunny windowsill, you can raise enough salad to feed a family of four for a year. You can "farm" twenty-five 4-inch pots in which you can grow:

- 5 or 6 kinds of herbs
- 20 to 30 carrots
- 30 to 35 beets
- All the radishes you can eat
- Even a few tomatoes

That windowsill space is a potential green mine. You can grow anything on a windowsill that requires a 1- or 2-inch spacing between plants, or single plants that keep producing an edible crop. This gives you a choice of four categories:

Sprouts: radish seeds, alfalfa seeds, mung beans, soybeans, wheat, buckwheat, and cress

Figure 3-1. Extraordinary ideas for vegetable containers.

Root vegetables: carrots, beets, green onions, and garlic

Herbs: chives, parsley, basil, dill, rosemary, sage, summer savory, tarragon, and sweet marjoram

Tomatoes: Tiny Tim is the most popular.

In an outside window box, you can grow almost anything. In window boxes, it's easiest to plant in pots and simply set the pots in the box. Most gardeners like to mix vegetables, herbs, and flowers in this setting (Figures 3-2 and 3-3).

Planting Your Patio

Whiskey barrel halves make great patio planters. They are 22 inches across, so they hold enough soil to support good vegetable growth. A single barrel will hold seven to eight corn plants, two or three zucchini plants, and two or three tomatoes. You can place them on wheels and roll them around the patio. Wheels can be purchased at any hardware store.

Figure 3-2. A variety of window box containers.

Figure 3-3. Large plant containers.

A wheelbarrow also works well (Figure 3-4).

Wooden boxes are also excellent for standard patio planting. Wood has a high insulation value and keeps the hot summer sun of most patio areas from drying the soil out rapidly and damaging the roots. You can buy these boxes from a garden center or make them. Boxes

Figure 3-4. A wheelbarrow makes a great container.

come in many sizes. Terra cotta pots also come in many shapes and sizes (Figure 3-5a-b).

Some gardeners like the paper pulp pots. They are easy to lift and fill with potting soil. We recommend using pots with either a 12-inch or an 18-inch inside diame-

ter, depending on what you want to plant. You can plant carrots and lettuce in 12-inch pots and eggplant, tomatoes, peppers, and other larger plants in 18-inch pots. Hanging wire baskets and containers also enhance any patio kitchen garden.

**Figure 3-5a.
Terra cotta pots.**

**Figure 3-5b.
Hanging planters.**

Eight Easy Steps

Follow these steps for planting your container vegetables:

1. Select an attractive container with drainage holes. If the container you select doesn't have holes, drill them.
2. Add commercial potting soil to within an inch of the top of the container. Use a planting mix with sphagnum peat moss.
3. Moisten the soil before planting.
4. You can plant both herbs and vegetables in the same container. When you plant them together, you can crowd them a little bit. An 18-inch pot, for instance, will easily hold as many as ten herbs.
5. If you are planting several vegetables and herbs together in the same container, set the taller varieties in the center.
6. Water to settle the soil around the roots.
7. Add more soil if it's needed after watering.
8. Keep the container moist and fertilized.

Container Soil Mixes

Container soil is a combination of organic materials (bark, compost, peat moss) and minerals. Any container mix must also provide the right nutrients for vegetable growth and enough air space (despite compacting) to allow good air and water movement. You can also grow vegetables in the commercial soilless mixes (such as Supersoil) since many of them contain all the ingredients necessary for good plant growth.

No-Mess Mixing

We hate the mess that sometimes occurs when you are gardening indoors or on a patio. If this is your problem, we have an answer. You'll need a 5-gallon plastic pail and a 1-quart kitchen measuring cup, along with a large wooden spoon and a plastic sheet to put over your work area to catch any spillage.

Mix your ingredients in the kitchen or work area sink. Moisten the contents with hot water to cut down on the dust. Stir slowly with the wooden spoon until everything is mixed.

Planting Seeds and Seedlings in Containers

When planting seeds in a container, you don't have to space them any particular distance apart. Simply scatter the seeds across the entire container. Later, however, you will have to thin the seedlings. Carrots, for instance, are thinned first to $^3/_4$ of an inch apart, then to 1 to 2 inches apart. You can throw the small carrots you're thinning into a soup or a stew, and you won't feel as if you're wasting anything. The 8-inch containers of carrots planted on a 1-inch spacing will produce the equivalent of a 5-foot row grown in an outdoor garden.

If you plant young seedlings in outdoor containers, you should get them used to outdoor conditions by taking them out in the morning and back inside at night. Gradually expose the seedlings to low temperatures and more sunlight for about two weeks or until you can leave them out without damage from frost.

No-Mess Watering Techniques

Watering your indoor containers shouldn't be any problem. Pots less than 8 inches in diameter should be watered from above with a 1-quart kitchen measuring cup. Another technique is to submerge the bottom half of the pot in a pail of water (or fill a kitchen sink). When the air bubbles stop coming up from the soil, take the pot out and let it drain. Large containers should be watered from above with a plastic pail, or a gentle stream from a hose, until the soil is completely saturated.

Don't water again until the soil is dry to a depth of 1 inch. To find out how dry the soil is, poke a finger into the soil, or take some soil from this depth and rub it between your thumb and index finger. If it's dry, water. If the soil is mud-coated or feels wet, it won't need water for at least twenty-four hours.

You should not let your containers dry out since vegetables must grow rapidly to maturity. If the plant is overwatered, the soil becomes waterlogged, forcing air from the soil and suffocating the plant. If at all possible, we suggest that you connect your containers with a drip system, put the whole thing on an automatic timer, and water each container with an emitter.

You can also buy large self-watering pots. They come in a number of shapes and sizes. These contain a built-in reservoir that gets filled through a slot in the side of the pot. During warm, dry weather, you need to refill these reservoirs once or twice a week. You can also fertilize these pots by adding fish emulsion directly to the water. Dump the water when it turn brackish.

Midget Fruits and Vegetables

If we didn't know better, we'd say that plant breeders developed the whole range of midget vegetables just for container gardeners. Over the last few years, a number of vegetables have been developed that are only half, even a fifth, the size of regular ones. The seed source codes listed throughout this book correspond with the codes in the Appendix.

Baby Gourmet Beets

To grow baby gourmet beets, scatter the seeds across an entire container. Cover with about $1/4$ inch of planter mix. Thin to stand 1 to 2 inches apart.

Gladiator: Crimson, gold ball-sized beet. Seed source: GUR

Little Ball: Smooth 1-inch ball. Seed source: BURP HIG ORN PAR PIN SEE SHE STO TER TIL TWI WILL

Baby Cabbage

Start the midget cabbages from seeds indoors in aluminum pans or peat pots about six to eight weeks before you intend to plant them in containers. For outdoor containers, plant midget cabbage about 4 inches apart. For windowsills or under lights, plant in 6-inch pots. Keep the temperature between 60° to 70°F.

Baby Early: A 2-pound, red, tight-headed cabbage. Seed source: COM

Badger Babyhead: 2- to 3-pound baby cabbage. Great flavor. Seed source: HEN

Baby Carrots

Plant baby carrots in the spring, and continue the planting throughout the summer. Plant 6 to 10 per each 4-inch pot. You can grow carrots in windowsill pots, under lights, or in larger containers outdoors.

Little Finger: Extra sweet, 3 to 4 inches long. A gourmet Nantes-type carrot. Seed source: BOU COM GUR JLH JUN ORN PIN VER

Short 'N' Sweet: A bright orange, 3-inch long carrot. Seed source: FAR LED

Baby Cauliflower

Start from seed indoors about six to eight weeks before you intend to plant in containers. For outdoor containers, plant midget cauliflower about 5 inches apart.

Garnat: White, 2- to 4-inch head. Seed source: THO

Baby Corn

Plant midget corn 5 inches apart in 12-inch or larger pots. Midget corn grows especially well in 5-gallon cans. Plant in the spring after your patio has warmed up. Make additional plantings every few weeks for a continuous harvest. You can also grow 5-gallon containers of midget corn behind a south-facing window.

Golden Midget: Yellow, 4-inch ears, 10 rows of kernels. Seed source: **ABU GAR SEED VER**

Baby Cucumbers

Plant these midget cucumbers in 6- to 8-inch pots, and cover with 1 inch of soil. You can plant in larger containers with 4-inch spacing between the plants. Place the containers out on the balcony or patio after the weather has warmed up in the spring.

Bush Pickle: 20- to 24-inch vine, dark green cucumber for pickling. Seed source: **BURP GUR HEN JUN LED LIB MEY PAR STO**

Patio Pic: 6 $^1/_2$-inch cucumbers. Seed source: **GLE**

Baby Eggplant

Plant seed $^1/_3$-inch deep in compressed peat pots. Plant pot and all in a 12-inch or larger container. Place in full sun, and don't move outdoors until the weather warms up in the spring.

Baby White Tiger: This is a tiny eggplant, 1 to 2 inches long. Seed source: **SEE**

Bambino: This eggplant is only 12 inches tall with small fruit. Seed source: **BURP GUR LIB SHE STO TER**

Early Black Egg: Shiny black fruit, 4-by-2-inch egg-shaped fruit. Seed source: **GAR GLE SOU**

Baby Lettuce

Plant baby lettuce directly in a container 4 to 5 inches apart. Midget lettuce grows well in 4-inch or larger pots and is especially popular for window box gardening. Make outdoor plantings every two weeks in separate small containers. Start 2 to 4 weeks before the last killing frost in the spring. Inside, plant anytime. You can easily grow lettuce on a windowsill or under lights.

Tom Thumb: Tennis ball–sized, medium green heads. Seed source: **GUR HEN HIG LED NIC ORG ORN PIN POR SEE SEED SHE SOU TIL VER**

Baby Melons/Pumpkins

Plant 3 seeds per 5-gallon container. When about 5 inches high, cut 2 of them out with a pair of scissors. Let the remaining plant grow to maturity.

Bush Musketeer: 3- to 4-pound melons, heavily netted, orange flesh. Seed source: HEN JUN MEY PAR STO

Bush Sugar Baby: An oval, 8- to 10-pound watermelon, scarlet flesh. Seed source: BURP BURR

Garden Baby: A round, 6- to 7-inch diameter watermelon. Grows on bush-type vines. Seed source: DEG VER

Munchkin: Bright orange, 3- to 4-inch flattened pumpkin. Good cooks like to stuff these little guys. Seed source: JUN SHE

Tomatoes

Start indoors 6 to 8 weeks before you intend to plant in your containers. If you're planting on a patio, don't move the seedlings outside until the weather has warmed up. These tomatoes will grow in 8- to 10-inch pots. See Figure 3-5.

Burpee's Pixie: Determinate plant that grows about 16 inches high. The fruit is $1^1/_4$-inches in diameter. Seed source: ALL PON TOM TOMA

Patio: This is a 24- to 26-inch plant. The fruit grows to about 2 inches in diameter. Seed source: ALL COM DEG LED LIB TOM TOMA WIL

Pixie Hybrid II: An 18-inch tall plant. Produces bright scarlet, $1^1/_2$-inch fruit. Seed source: JUN ORN TOMA WIL

Tiny Tim: This really is a tiny plant that grows to about 6 inches tall. It produces $1/_4$-inch bright red tomatoes. Seed source: ALL BURG COM GLE LED SEE STO TOM TOMA WILL

Baby Zucchini

Plant 2 to 3 plants in a 10-gallon container. Wrap your container with a wire cage to help support the plant.

Ambassador: Pick the green fruit when it is small. Seed source: COM LEB MEY PIN WIL

Golden Dawn II: Golden yellow fruit. Pick when small. Seed source: GAR PAR

Chapter Four

Gardening to Eat Well

More than ever before, good cooks try to combine delicious foods with mealtime creativity, a creativity that has placed new emphasis on the fresh taste and appearance of basic ingredients. This often means using super-fresh vegetables and herbs that impart just the right flavor to any meal. It also means growing interesting and unusual varieties that you won't find in local supermarkets.

The following vegetables and herbs make a good starting place for the cook who likes to innovate. You can grow all of these in your garden or just one. Karen has what we call an experimental garden bench near our kitchen where she tries new varieties in large pots. This year she has Lemon and Spicy Globe basil, Italian Gold Sauce tomatoes, and a few other new varieties. Next year, the best-flavored varieties will show up in our regular garden.

Vegetables

As you begin your kitchen garden, we suggest that you stick to these fifteen standard vegetables:

Green beans	Carrots
Beets	Corn
Broccoli	Cucumbers
Eggplant	Radishes
Lettuce	Scallions
Peas	Squash
Peppers	Potatoes
	Tomatoes

Among each of these fifteen vegetables, you will find many variations in taste, color, and texture.

We also recommend that you start with a basic herb garden that includes rosemary, oregano, thyme, and parsley. This can be as simple as four pots on the windowsill, a few herbs planted in a flower bed, or herbs stuck into the corners of your regular garden beds. After you've established these herbs, you can see what your recipes call for and plant additional ones.

Good cooks are always looking for the choicest, freshest possible vegetables and ingredients for meals, and they know that the most interesting varieties and seasonal tastes are not always found in supermarkets. Today's cooking calls for a variety of shapes, colors, and textures to enhance the appearance of every dish. In the first section of this chapter, we will look at some of the more interesting varieties available to the gourmet gardener, as well as the standard varieties most cooks know and depend on.

Beans

Pole Beans (Green)

Fine grocery stores and produce markets everywhere are advertising the Blue Lake Pole bean as a gourmet green bean. It has a tasty, succulent, and mild nutlike flavor. All green beans, of course, are delicious served with a tomato sauce, cooked with garlic, or just cooked plain.

Blue Lake: 6-foot plant produces 6-inch long green beans. Can be used fresh, canned, or frozen. Seed source: **ABU ALL BOU BURG BURR GAR GUR HEN JLH JUN PAR PON POR ROS SEE SHE STO TER THO TIL VER WILL**

Kentucky Wonder: This 1850s heirloom variety is a hardy climber. Beans are stringless, meaty, and tender with fine flavor and texture. Good fresh, canned, or frozen. Seed source: **ABU ALL BURG BURR BUT COM DEG FAR GAR GUR HEN HIG MEY NIC ORG PIN POR ROS SEE SEED SOU STO TER THO TIL VER WIL WILL**

Pole Beans (Yellow and Purple)

Kentucky Wonder Wax Round Pod: 7- to 9-inch pods are waxy yellow. Almost stringless. Seed source: **ALL COM GUR HEN JUN MEY STO VER**

Louisiana Purple Pod: Bright purple 7-inch pods that should be picked when young and stringless. Seed source: **ABU PIN SOU**

Bush Beans (Green)

These are bush varieties that grow up to 12 inches high. No support is necessary.

Blue Lake Bush: 18-inch plant. $6^1/_2$-inch dark green pods are stringless. Seed source: **ABU ALL BURR DEG FIS HIG MEY ORN POR ROS STO TIL**

Kentucky Wonder: Bush version of Kentucky Wonder pole. 8-inch pods that need to be kept picked to induce a huge yield. Seed source: **GUR PAR SEE THO VER**

Roma II: This Italian Romano-type bean is $4^1/_2$-inches, flat, and medium green. Use fresh, canned, or frozen. Seed source: **BURP COM JUN LED MEY ORN PAR POR TWI VER WIL**

Triomphe De Farcy: 18-inch plant. 3- to 7-inch long, $1/2$-inch wide, straight, thin pod has purple mottling. This is an heirloom variety. Seed source: **BURP COO GOU JOH LEJ**

Bush Beans (Wax)

Beurre De Rocquencourt: 16-inch plant. 6-7-inch stringless yellow pods. Seed source: **ABU GAR GOU PIN SEE SEED TER WILL**

Mini Yellow: Pick 4-inch pods, as they are mature. Use fresh, frozen, canned, or even pickled. Seed source: **PAR**

Bush Beans (Purple)

Royal Burgundy: 12- to 15-inch plant. 6-inch purple pods turn green when cooked. These beans are pretty on the plant. Use fresh or frozen. Seed source: **BURP COM COO DEG GUR HEN JUN LED SEE SHE STO TER TIL TWI VER WILL**

Lima Beans (Pole)

However they grow, you love them or you hate them.

King of the Garden: This is a long-season producer. Climbs to 10 feet tall. 5- to 8-inch dark green pods are good for shelling or freezing. Pale green, thick, and flat beans. Seed source: **COM DEG GUR JUN LED MEY PAR PON RED SEE SOU STO TWI VER**

Lima Beans (Bush)

Fordhook 242: 3- to 4-inch pods produce plump seeds. Use fresh, canned, or frozen. Seed source: **ALL BURP BURR COM DEG GUR HEN JOH JUN LED MEY ORN PAR PON POR SEE STO TWI VER WIL**

Henderson Bush: 1889 heirloom variety has 3-inch flat, dark green pods that produce small seeds. Use fresh, canned, or frozen. Seed source: **ALL BURP GUR MEY PAR PIN POR ROS SEE TWI VER WIL**

Dried Beans

Why dried beans? Because there are so many wonderful beans never found in regular markets today:

Appaloosa, Black Valentine, Vermont, Cranberry, and others. Dried beans are versatile. They can be baked, boiled, or refried. You can combine cooked dried beans with vegetables, ham hocks, smoked sausage, or rice. Some varieties are good served with cornbread and cooked greens; others are good made into bean soups or dips. And don't forget the refried beans with hot spices added as a mainstay for Mexican burritos.

Fava Beans

Broad Long Pod: 7-inch long, oblong, flat, light-green pod. Seed source: ALL BURP COO PLA POR SOU SUN VER

Kidney Beans

Red Kidney: 20- to 22-inch tall plant produces large, flat green pods with pinkish red to mahogany beans. Seed source: ALL BUT COM DEG FAR GAR GUR HEN LED PAR PON VER WILL

Miscellaneous Beans

Appaloosa: Like the horse with the spots on its rump, the white beans are mottled maroon and black. A bushy plant that has runners. Seed source: ABU PLA

Black Bean: These tiny black beans are used extensively in Mexican cooking. Seed source: JLH

Maine Yellow Eye: Light green pod has plump, yellow tan beans with a squashlike flavor. Good baking bean. 18-inch plant. Seed source: ABU ALL GAR JOH ORG RED SEE SOU VER

Navy: Small white seeds that are used in bean soup. Seed source: COM GAR LED SEE VER

Pinto: 5-inch pods have seeds that are light buff speckled with greenish brown. This variety is also used in Mexican cooking. Seed source: ABU DEG HEN LED PAR PIN POR SEE VER WILL

Santa Maria Pinquito: A pink, square bean. Seed source: NIC RED SEE SOU

Scotch: Aptly named for its butterscotch color. Seed source: ABU

Vermont Cranberry Bush: Heirloom soup bean has maroon seed with rose tan streaks. Tastes like steak, which makes it a good meat substitute. Seed source: COO PIN RED VER

Beets

Beets make an excellent crop for kitchen gardens because it's possible to grow a large quantity in a small space. Beets range in color from red to white to yellow, and in shapes from semi-globe to cylindrical.

Detroit Dark Red: 3-inch diameter, dark red beet. Good fresh, canned, or frozen. Seed source: ABU ALL BURP BURR DEG FAR GAR GUR HEN LEJ ORG PIN PON POR SEE SEED SOU STO TIL TWI VER WIL WILL

Chioggia: This Italian heirloom variety has a candy red exterior and rings of cherry red and creamy white interior. Beautiful beet. Seed source: COO JOH NIC ORN PIN SEE SEED SHE SOU

Cylindra: Grows up to 8 inches long, 2 to 3 inches across. Good slicer. Dark red beet. Seed source: BURP BURR COM FAR FIS GAR GOU HEN JUN PAR PIN PON SEE SHE TIL TWI WILL

Golden Beet: Small, round golden beet. Good pickler. Seed source: ABU BURP COO FIS GLE GUR HIG JUN LED NIC ORN PIN PON SEE SHE STO SOU WILL

Little Ball: The mini beet for small gardens. Red 3-inch diameter ball forms rapidly, but should be picked when $1^1/_2$-inches in diameter. Plant densely in succession for crops all season. Seed source: BURP HIG ORN PAR PIN SHE STO TER TIL TWI WILL

Snowwhite: Pure white, 1- to 3-inch roots. Good pickler with extra sweet flavor. Seed source: COO GOU ORN SEE STO TER

Broccoli

Some broccoli varieties put out lots of side branches (called shoots) in addition to a main head. Others have a central head but produce few side branches; still others produce side branches but no central head. The best for small gardens are the varieties that produce good-sized central heads and lots of side branches.

There are also different colors and related varieties that make a wonderful addition to the garden and table, such as Romanesco, which is a chartreuse, spiral-shaped variety.

Calabrese: 3-foot plant produces a 6-inch diameter head. Has lots of side shoots. Use fresh or frozen. Seed source: ABU BOU FAR JLH NIC PIN RED SEE SOU

Green Comet: 9-inch central head; few side shoots. Good fresh or frozen. Seed source: BURP COM COO FAR GUR HEN JUN LED LIB MEY PAR PIN PON POR THO TWI VER WILL

Waltham 29: 8-inch slate green head on compact plant. Plenty of side shoots. Seed source: ABU ALL BURR BUT COM DEG LED LIB MEY ROS SEE SOU TIL

Other Types/Colors

Early Purple Sprouting: 3-foot plant with medium-sized head. Purple head that turns green when cooked. Seed source: ABU BOU THO

Romanesco: 3-foot plant should be caged to keep from blowing over in the wind. Beautiful plant with conical spirals that has loads of little apple green spears that can be snapped off individually or together. Seed source: ABU BOU JLH LEJ NIC ORN SEE SHE THO

White Sprouting: This 3-foot plant is a heavy cropper. Small, white head looks like cauliflower. Good for freezing. Seed source: BOU

Carrots

Carrots are a staple in the Newcomb garden. We grow all sizes and shapes and harvest the entire year (Figure 4-1). There is nothing like fresh carrots just pulled and eaten raw, or dropped in the pot as an ingredient in stews and soups.

Danvers Half Long: 1871 heirloom variety. 8 by 2 inches and nearly coreless. Seed source: ALL BURP DEG FAR FIS GAR GUR HEN LEJ MEY PIN PON ROS SEE SOU THO TIL WILL

Imperator: The type you'd find in grocery stores. Grows 10 inches long and $1^1/_2$- inches thick. Seed source: BURP FAR LED MEY PON ROS VER

Little Finger: A tiny Nantes type, 3 by $^5/_8$ inches with a small core and

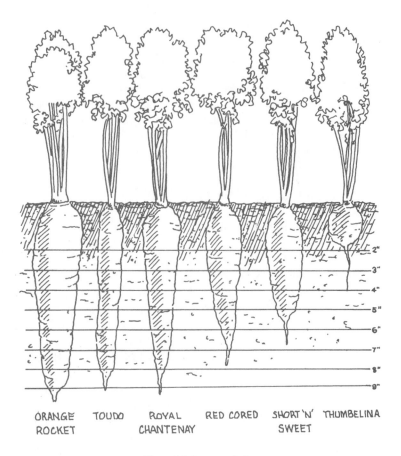

ORANGE TOUDO ROYAL RED CORED SHORT 'N' THUMBELINA
ROCKET   CHANTENAY   SWEET

Figure 4-1. Carrot varieties.

extra-sweet taste. Excellent small space variety. Seed source: BOU COM GUR JLH JUN ORN PIN VER

Nantes: 6 by $1^1/_2$ inches, red hue. Seed source: COM DEG HEN LEJ MEY ORG PIN SEE SEED

Red-Cored Chantenay: 6-by-2-inch red orange carrot that keeps its rich color when cooked. Seed source: ABU DEG FAR FIS GAR GUR HEN JUN MEY NIC PIN PON ROS SEED SOU TIL WIL WILL

Thumbelina: This tiny carrot is $^1/_2$-inch round in diameter. The roots are smooth and tasty. It's perfect for small spaces. Seed source: ALL BURP COM COO FAR GAR GUR JOH JUN LED NIC PAR PIN POR STO TWI WILL

Corn

Today's corn is sweeter than ever, and the sweetness lasts longer after picking. This sweetness is in the genes. "Sugar-enhanced" corn has a gene (labeled "SE") that modifies the normal gene for sweetness. Each tasty kernel has a higher sugar content than normal corn, which makes them tender and sweeter. The *Supersweet* varieties (shrunken gene types SH2) have two or three times the content of normal sugary types. Many gardening cooks love the supersweet and use it often when corn is called for. Others say that it is too sweet and that sugar-enhanced types are better. Both sugar-enhanced and supersweet corn come in yellow, white, and bicolor varieties. Of course, you shouldn't restrict the corn you plant to these two types; don't forget standard varieties. If you prefer the supersweet varieties, you must isolate them from the regular corn.

Sugar-Enhanced Corn (SE Gene)

Divinity: 6-foot stalk, 9-inch ears, 16 rows of white kernels. Seed source: LIB STO

Early Xtra-Sweet: 6-foot stalk grows 9-inch ears with 12 to 16 rows of yellow kernels. Seed source: BURP FAR GOU GUR HEN PON VER WILL

Miracle: $6^1/_2$-foot stalk, $9^1/_2$-inch ears, 20 to 22 rows of yellow kernels. Seed source: BURP BURR COM FAR GOU GUR HIG LIB NIC STO TER WILL

Sugar and Gold: 7-foot stalk, $8^1/_2$-inch ears, 16 to 18 rows of yellow and white kernels. Seed source: COM FAR GUR

Supersweet Corn (SH2 Gene)

How Sweet It Is: 7-foot stalk, 8-inch ears, 16 rows white kernels. Seed source: GUR HEN JUN LED MEY NIC ORN PAR PIN POR TIL TWI VER WIL

Illini Gold Extra Sweet: $6^1/_2$-foot stalk, 8-inch ears, 14 to 18 rows of yellow kernels. Seed source: BURP DEG FAR GUR HEN JUN MEY VER WIL

Ivory and Gold: 6-foot stalk, 9-inch ears, 16 rows of yellow and white kernels. Seed source: STO VER

Corn (Standard)

Early Sunglow: $4^1/_2$-foot stalk, 7-inch ears, 12 rows of yellow kernels. Seed source: BURP BURR FAR FIS GUR HEN MEY NIC PAR POR SHE SOU TIL VER WIL

Golden Bantam: $6^1/_2$-foot stalk, 7-inch ears, 8 rows of yellow kernels. Seed source: ABU ALL BOU BURR BUT GAR GUR HEN JOH LED ORG SEE SOU WIL

Honey and Cream: $7^1/_2$-inch ears, 12 to 14 rows of yellow and white kernels. Seed source: ALL BURP GUR LIB PIN PON WIL

Platinum Lady: 7-foot stalk, 8-inch ears, 14 to 16 rows of white kernels. Seed source: BURP BURR COM GAR GUR MEY NIC ORN PIN STO TIL TWI VER

Space-Saver Corn

Golden Midget: 3-foot stalk, 4-inch ears, 10 rows of yellow kernels. Seed source: ABU GAR SEED VER

Popcorn

It's almost impossible to resist the taste of freshly popped corn, especially if you have grown it yourself. Nearly everyone serves popcorn the same way. We'd urge you to try tossing it with spices and seasonings, including cashews, chow mein noodles, ginger, and soy sauce. This gives it a crunchy, nutty taste. The color of the kernels of various varieties ranges from yellow to white to purple and rusty red. Here are some varieties to try.

South American Yellow Giant: 7-foot stalk, 8-inch ears with butter yellow kernels. Seed source: GUR LED MEY SEE

Strawberry Ornamental Popcorn: 4-foot stalk, 2-inch ears with mahogany kernels. Seed source: ALL COM COO GOU GUR HEN JLH JOH LED LIB MEY NIC PAR PLA SEE SHE SOU STO TIL TWI VER WIL

White Hull-Less: 6-foot stalk, 5-inch ears with plenty of white kernels. Seed source: BURR DEG LIB PIN PON STO TWI WILL

Cucumbers

Some cucumbers seem to be made for a small garden. Bush varieties thrive in a container and produce plenty of sweet, juicy fruit. Great for cucumber relish, cucumbers and sour cream, shrimp and cucumber canapes, chicken and cucumber mold, and more.

Bush Champion: This bushy plant produces 12-inch-long, bright green fruit. Seed source: BURP PON THO

Pot Luck: Grows well in containers and produces about 24, 7-inch fruits. Seed source: COM DEG MEY ORN WIL

Salad Bush: 8-inch-long fruit borne on compact plant. Seed source: BURP COM DEG HEN JUN LED LIB NIC PAR PIN POR SHE TIL TWI VER WILL

Spacemaster: 6-inch-long, dark green fruit. Seed source: ALL COM DEG FIS GAR GUR LIB ORN PIN PLA POR SEE TIL TWI VER WILL

Straight 8: 8-inch, white-spined cucumber with small seed cavity. Seed source: ABU ALL BURP COM DEG FAR FIS GUR HEN MEY POR SEE VER WIL WILL

Eggplant

Eggplant varieties vary in size, color, and texture. The fruits range from deep purple to lavender, red, green white, and hues in between. The standard eggplant is bell-shaped, plump, and roundish. Asian eggplants are long and slender. Garden cooks will want to try sage-grilled eggplant, eggplant a la Creole (sliced eggplant with Parmesan cheese), and other eggplant dishes that show off the individual varieties.

Bell-Shaped Eggplant

Black Beauty: 24- to 28-inch plant. Dark purple fruit has a small seed cavity. Seed source: ABU

ALL BURP BURR BUT COM DEG
GUR HEN LED LEJ MEY ORN PON
POR RED ROS SEE SOU VER WIL
WILL

Asian Type Eggplant
Ichiban: 36- to 40-inch plant.
Fruit grows to 12 inches long. Seed
source: BURR COM DEG GUR LED
PAR PIN POR TWI VER

Small Eggplant
Bambino: Grows only 12 inches
tall and produces tiny bell-shaped
fruit. Seed source: BURP GUR LIB
SHE STO TER

Early Black Egg: 4-by-2-inch,
shiny black fruit on bushy plant. Seed
source: GAR GLE SOU

Other Colors
Asian Bride: 5 to 7 inches
long with white skin streaked
with lavender. Seed source: COO
SHE

Italian Pink Bicolor: 8 inches, bell-shaped, creamy and rosy
pink. Seed source: SEED STO

Listada De Gandia: 6 to
10 inches long, white with

purple stripes. Seed source: ORN
SEE SEED SOU

White Egg: White and
the size of a hen's egg. Seed
source: SEE

Lettuce
Even though lettuce will be fully
explored in the next chapter, this is a
good place to begin thinking of what
varieties you might want to start with.
We don't restrict growing lettuce in
our ground garden, but grow head lettuce in pots on a covered patio during
the heat of our California summers.
Lettuce is very adaptable to hanging
baskets or pots, and to growing with a
flower or two. Lettuce comes in all
shapes, colors, and textures, and when
added to a salad bowl makes for an irre-
sistible part of any meal.

Head Lettuce
Great Lakes: Large, bright green,
dense head. Seed source: ALL BURP
COM DEG HEN MEY NIC PIN SEE TIL

Buttercrunch/Bibb Lettuce
Buttercrunch: Smooth, dark
green leaves form a 6-inch-wide

rosette center. Seed source: ABU ALL BOU BURP BURR BUT COM COO DEG FAR FIS GUR HEN HIG JOH JUN LED LIB MEY NIC PAR PIN PON POR ROS SEE SOU STO TER TIL VER WIL WILL

Marvel of 4 Seasons: Wavy green leaves with ruby tips. Seed source: COO GOU HIG JLH ORG ORN PIN RED SEE SEED SHE TER

Susan's Red Bibb: Ruffled leaves with rose margins. Seed source: SOU

Space-Saving Lettuce

Little Gem: Miniature romaine with bright green slightly wavy leaves. 5 to 6 inches tall. Seed source: BOU GAR ORN PAR SEED TER

Tom Thumb: Tennis ball–sized buttercrunch with medium green, crumpled leaves. Seed source: GUR HEN HIG LED NIC ORG ORN PIN POR SEE SEED SHE SOU TIL VER

Loose-leaf Lettuce

Oak Leaf: Medium green leaves look like oak leaves. Seed source: ABU ALL BURG BUT COM DEG FAR FIS GAR GOU GUR HEN HIG JLH JOH LED LIB MEY NIC ORN PIN PON POR RED SEE SOU VER

Red Oak Leaf: Deeply indented crimson, cranberry, or burgundy leaves. Seed source: ORN SEE SHE

Salad Bowl: Wavy, light green, deeply lobed leaves. Seed source: ABU ALL BOU BURP BURR BUT COM COO DEG FAR FIS GAR GUR HEN HIG JOH JUN LED LIB MEY NIC ORN PAR PIN SEE SOU TER TIL WIL WILL

Romaine Lettuce

Parris Island Cos: 8 to 9 inches tall with dark green leaves. Seed source: BURP COM GAR HEN JOH LIB MEY PIN POR RED SEE SEED SOU STO TIL VER WIL WILL

Rouge D'Hiver: Broad, flat, bronze to deep red leaves. Seed source: COO JLH ORN SEE SEED SHE

Edible Pod Peas

Snap peas, with their thick, crunchy pods have become today's gourmet pea found in most specialty markets. They are delicious with basil and lemon, creamed with carrots, or combined with peppers. Throw them in a stir-fry or eat them plain. Snap peas, however, vary widely in flavor. Some are sweet; others have little taste. We suggest you try a number of the varieties in your kitchen garden and judge for yourself.

Mammoth Melting Sugar: 4- to 5-foot vine, 4-by-$^7/_8$-inch pods. Seed source: ABU BURP COM DEG GOU HEN HIG RED SEE VER

Sugar Ann: 18-inch vine, space saver. Seed source: ABU BURG GAR GOU HEN HIG JOH JUN LED MEY NIC PIN PON POR STO SUN TER TWI WILL

Sugar Daddy: 30-inch vine. Seed source: BOU COO GUR HEN JUN LED PAR STO TER TWI VER

Sugar Mel: 24-inch vine, 3- to 4-inch pods. Seed source: BURR FIS GAR ORN PAR PIN SHE SOU

Sugar Snap: 6-foot vine, 3-inch pods. Seed source: ABU ALL BOU BURG BURP BURR BUT COM DEG GAR GUR HEN HIG JOH JUN LED MEY NIC PAR PLA POR RED ROS SEE SOU SUN TIL TWI VER WIL WILL

Regular Peas
Bush Peas

Little Marvel: 18-inch vine, 3-inch pods, with 7 to 9 peas per pod. Seed source: ABU ALL BURP BURR DEG FAR GUR HEN JUN LED MEY PON POR SEE SOU STO TIL WIL WILL

Novella: 20- to 25-inch vine, semileafless variety. 3-inch pods. Seed source: COM COO GUR JUN PAR POR WILL

Tall Peas

Alaska: $2^1/_2$-inch pods with 6 to 8 peas per pod. Seed source: ABU BURR BUT DEG FAR MEY PIN SEE TIL VER WIL

Alderman: 4- to 6-foot vine, 5-inch pods, 8 to 9 peas per pod. Seed source: ABU ALL BOU COM FAR GAR LED ORN PIN SEE STO TER TIL VER WILL

Peppers

Good cooks often use peppers in their cooking like an artist's pallet. Peppers come in bright red, yellow, shiny green, orange, and purple colors that add an exciting look to any dish. Golden bells look especially attractive stuffed with sausage, onion, and cheese. Here are some varieties you might like to try. Hot peppers will be covered in Chapters 7 and 9.

Green Peppers

Bell Boy: $3^1/_4$-by-$3^1/_2$-inch glossy green pepper. 24-inch plant. Seed source: COM DEG FAR GUR HEN JUN LED MEY PIN STO TOMA VER WIL WILL

Emerald Giant: $4^1/_2$-by-$4^1/_2$-inch pepper, 4 lobes, thick walls. Seed source: BURR DEG ORN SEE TIL TWI

Red Peppers

Earliest Red Sweet: 3-by-4-inch pepper, 2 to 3 lobes, bright red when ripe. Seed source: HIG PIN STO

Sweet Red Cherry: 1-inch-long, flattened globe, bright red when ripe. 18-inch plant. Seed source: LIB NIC VER

Yellow/Orange Peppers

Golden Bell: 4-by-$3^1/_2$-inch pepper, 3 to 4 lobes, golden color when mature. Seed source: COM MEY PIN TER VER WIL

Gypsy: $4^1/_2$-by-$2^1/_4$-inch pepper. Thick, pale yellow walls. 16- to 20-inch plant. Seed source: BURP COM FAR GUR HEN JUN LED LIB NIC ORN PAR PIN POR TER TOMA VER WILL

Orange Grande: $5^1/_2$ inches, ripens to orange when mature. Seed source: STO

Other Colors

Chocolate Bell: $4^1/_2$ inches long, 3 to 4 lobes. Turns from tan to dark red when ripe. Seed source: BOU BURP COO HIG JOH PAR SEE SOU STO TOMA

Ivory Charm: Blocky, 4 lobes, from creamy white to pastel yellow when ripe. Seed source: SHE

Potatoes

Cooks often love to mix different colored potatoes together in a potato salad just for the visual effect or show them off in such dishes as shrimp-stuffed potatoes. Potatoes can easily be grown in a postage stamp garden. We grow ours inside old tires stacked two high and filled with compost. In one set we plant blue potatoes, in the second we plant yellow, and in the third we plant white potatoes. What fun it is to pull up these different-colored tubers. The tires store heat and allow us to plant a little earlier than normal.

White Potatoes

Kennebec: Large, oval potatoes that are best planted closer than 10 inches. Seed source: BURP FAR GUR HEN JOH JUN LED MEY TIL

Red Skin Potatoes

Red Pontiac: Round potato with shallow eyes. Seed source: BURP FAR GUR HEN JUN LED MEY

Blue Potatoes

All Blue Potato: Blue skin, blue flesh. Seed source: GUR HEN PAR SHE TER

Lavender: Lavender skin and flesh. Seed source: SEE

Other Colors

Cherries Jubilee: Small, rounded, with bright cherry pink skin and pale pink flesh. Seed source: SHE

Fingerlings: 1-inch-long potato, yellow skin, yellow flesh. Seed source: JUN SEE

Yukon Gold: Yellow flesh. Seed source: BURP COO FIS GAR GUR HEN JOH LED SEE TIL

Radishes

No vegetable grows faster than a radish. As with most vegetables, radishes come in all sizes, shapes, and colors. If you mix carrot and radish seeds together and scatter them across a bed at the approximate spacing for carrots, the radishes will come up first and mark the bed. You'll be able to harvest the radishes shortly before the baby carrots need thinning.

Looking for variety in a package? Try one of the gourmet radish blends on the market. Northrup King prepackages Early Scarlet globe, French Breakfast, Sparkler, and White Icicle all in one package. Scatter the seeds across the bed, and cover with about $1/4$ inch of planting mix. Your salad radish selection will be ready to harvest in about 21 days.

Burpee also prepackages a trio of Cherry Belle, French Breakfast, and White Icicle.

Red, Round Radishes

Cherry Belle: $^3/_4$-inch radish that resembles a cherry. Seed source: **ABU ALL BOU BURP BURR COM DEG FAR FIS GUR HEN JUN LED LEJ LIB MEY NIC PIN PON POR SEE SEED SOU STO TIL TWI VER WIL WILL**

White Tip Radishes

Sparkler: $1^3/_4$-inch-long, scarlet radish with a white tip. Seed source: **BURR DEG FAR FIS GAR HEN JUN LEJ LIB MEY NIC PON POR ROS SEE STO WIL WILL**

All-White Radishes

White Icicle: 4 to 5 inches long and all white. Seed source: **ALL BURG BURP BURR COM DEG FAR FIS GAR GUR HEN JLH JUN LED LIB MEY NIC ORN PIN PON POR SEE SOU STO TER TWI VER WIL WILL**

Other Colors

Easter Egg: Round, red, pin, white, purple, and violet. Seed source: **BURP COM COO GAR GUR HEN JOH JUN LIB NIC ORN PAR PIN POR SHE TER TIL VER WILL**

Scallions

Scallions are so much easier to grow than onions.

He Ski Ko Evergreen: White, pungent flesh without bulbs. Seed source: **ALL BOU COM FAR GUR HEN JLH JUN NIC PIN SEE STO THE VER**

Red Welch Bunching: 14-inch-long, red, bulbless onions grow in clusters. Seed source: **VER**

Squash

Even though squash is classified as summer and winter, both are grown at the same time of year. The difference is that summer squash are harvested and eaten during the summer. Summer squash vary widely in shape and color, but all have much the same mild taste. Summer squash includes straightneck, curved neck, scallop, and zucchini. Winter squash are left on the vine so their rinds can harden, and they are not harvested until late fall, so they can be stored throughout the winter months.

Sunburst Squash

Sunburst looks like a plump patty pan squash, but has a creamy white flesh and mild flavor. Harvest at any size. Sunburst is bright yellow, even when small, and can be harvested before the blossoms fall off and served with stir-fry greens. Stuff the mature fruit with rice and hamburger, chopped ham and cheese, and other similar combinations.

Plant in the spring when the soil warms up. Space 28 inches apart. Keep watered. They'll be ready to harvest in 6 to 8 weeks. Squash bugs don't seem to favor this variety.

Seed source: COM DEG GAR JOH LIB NIC ORN PAR PIN POR SHE TER VER

Scallop Squash

A 2- to 4-inch-diameter squash that looks like a scalloped spaceship.

Peter Pan: Pale green scallop rind, pale green flesh. Seed source: BOU BURG BURR ORG SEE

Sunburst: Pick when 3 inches across. Bright golden yellow. Seed source: COM DEG GAR JOH LIB NIC ORN PAR PIN POR SHE TER VER

Straightneck Squash

8- to 12-inch-long, 2- to 4-inch-wide, straight yellow squash.

Early Prolific Straightneck: Harvest creamy yellow squash at 3 to 4 inches long. Seed source: ALL BURP BURR BUT COM DEG FIS GAR GUR HEN LED MEY ROS SOU VER WIL

Park's Creamy: 6-inch yellow straightneck (a space-saver variety) 18-inch plant. Seed source: PAR

Crookneck Squash

8- to 12-inch-long, 2- to 4-inch-wide, yellow squash that has a curve at the neck.

Golden Spice: Golden yellow crookneck (a space-saver variety). Seed source: LIB

Yellow Crookneck: Bright yellow fruit should be picked when 4 to 5 inches long. Seed source: BUT GAR HIG JOH ORG PIN SEE SEED SOU TER

Zucchini

Zucchini originated in South America and came to Italy with the early explorers. Once zucchini arrived, Italian cooks practically turned it into a national vegetable. Zucchini, in Italy (and more recently in America), is marinated, grilled, dipped in batter and fried, stuffed, and more. Gold Slice, Green Magic II, and Park's creamy are good space savers.

Dark Green Zucchini: Pick when 6 to 7 inches long. Seed source: ABU DEG GAR JLH LIB RED ROS SOU WILL

Burpee Golden: Bright golden yellow zucchini. Seed source: BURP

French White Bush: 3 to 5 inches long. Seed source: NIC SEE

Kuta: Pick this light green fruit before it's 6 inches long. Low in calories and fat. Seed source: PAR

Zucchini Round: Bright yellow fruit on bushy plant. Seed source: DEG

Green Magic II: Dark green zucchini on compact, 18-inch plant (a space-saver variety). Seed source: PAR

Winter Squash

Unlike summer squash, only the flesh of winter squash is edible. The seeds can also be harvested and roasted. Winter squash varies from mostly sweet to mild, from fibrous to creamy flesh. Some types and varieties to try include Bush Buttercup, Butternut Bush, Cream of the Crop, Early Butternut, and Little Gem; they will also save you space.

 Ebony (acorn): 5-by-6-inch squash. Stores well. Seed source: BOU BURR BUT COM HIG JOH JUN LED LEJ LIB ORG PIN SHE TER VER

Jersey Golden Acorn: Golden rind, light orange meat. Semibush plant. Seed source: BURP ORN

Cream of the Crop: 3-pound acorn squash with creamy white rind and pale flesh (a space-saver variety).

Buttercup: 3 to 5 pounds, $4^1/_2$ by $6^1/_2$ inches. Dark green rind with silvery white stripes. Thick, orange flesh. Seed source: ABU ALL BURP BURR COM DEG FAR FIS GAR GUR HEN JOH JUN LIB NIC PIN PON

SEE SEED SOU STO TER TIL TWI VER WILL

Bush Buttercup: 3 to 5 pounds, round, thick orange flesh (a space-saver variety). Seed source: ALL COM FIS Seed source: BUR COM FAR JOU JUN LIB PAR POR TER TWI WIL

Butternut Waltham: $3^1/_2$ by 9 inches, 3 to 5 pounds. Creamy tan rind, deep orange flesh. Seed source: ABU BOU BURP BURR COM DEG FAR GOU GUR HEN JOH JUN LED LIB ORG PAR PIN PON ROS SEE SEED SOU STO TWI VER WIL WILL

Butternut Bush: 10 to 12 inches long. Rich orange flesh (a space-saver variety). Seed source: PON

Early Butternut: 7 inches long. Rich orange flesh (a space-saver variety). Seed source: COM FAR HEN JUN LIB NIC PAR PIN POR STO TWI VER WIL WILL

Golden Hubbard: 10 by 9 inches, slightly warted, reddish orange rind with grayish stripes, yellow orange flesh. Seed source: ALL DEG GAR ORN PIN PON SEE STO TIL TWI VER WILL

Little Gem: 3 to 5 pounds, miniature Golden Hubbard type (a space-saver variety): Seed source: GLE.

Delicata: 8 by 3 inches, 1 to 2 pounds, creamy yellow with dark green stripes. Vining type sweet potato squash. Seed source: ABU BOU DEG GAR GUR HEN JOH JUN ORG PIN PLA PON SEE TER

Vegetable Spaghetti: A staple in our yearly garden. 3 to 4 pounds, oblong squash with yellow rind. It's low in calories and fat and is an excellent substitute for spaghetti. Seed source: ABU BURG BURP BURR BUT COM FIS GAR GLE GUR HEN HIG JOH JUN LED LIB ORG PAR PIN PLA PON POR RED ROS SEE SEED SOU STO TIL TWI VER WIL WILL

Tomatoes

More and more tomatoes are finding their way into gourmet cooking. Ripe tomatoes can be yellow green, orange, yellow, or multicolored and come in an array of sizes.

Some cooks literally go crazy with the surplus tomatoes from their kitchen garden. They whip up tomato dumplings, scalloped tomato casserole, herbed tomato-cheese bread, fried herb tomatoes, and much more.

The redder the tomato, the more tasty and tangy it is. People who can't tolerate red tomatoes because of acid may want to try the yellow and white nonacid tomatoes.

If you live in an area where tomatoes sometimes don't ripen until August, try a cold-tolerant cultivar such as Gem State, Oregon Spring, Sprint, Stokesalaska, Subarctic Maxi, and Subarctic Plenty. Each will set fruit at much lower temperatures. Most of these are determinate (they have limited growth) and bushy, making them a good choice for almost any kitchen garden.

Try also the compact dwarf indeterminate varieties. They're perfect for a small kitchen garden. They stay a compact 4 feet tall and have a strong central stem that can be tied to a short stake or caged in wire. Here are some interesting varieties.

Better Bush: 3- to 4-inch bright red fruit on a short bush. Seed Source: PAR

Evergreen Tomato: Indeterminate variety that remains green when ripe and has low acidity. Seed source: GLE SEE TOM TOMA

Husky Gold: 5- to 7-ounce fruit with orange interior. Seed source: BURP LED LIB MEY POR STO THO TOM TOMA TWI VER

Husky Red: Dark red tomato on compact plant. Seed source: LED LIB PAR STO TOM TOMA VER

Lemon Girl: 3 to 4 inches in diameter, bright yellow fruit. Seed source: BURP DEG HEN JLH LIB NIC PAR POR STO TER TOM TOMA VER WIL

Mr. Stripey: Red and yellow striped fruit. Seed source: ABU GLE JLH SEE SEED THO TOM TOMA

White Beauty: 8 ounces, ivory skin, and paper white flesh. Seed source: BURG FAR GLE SEE SOU TOM TOMA

Herbs

Along with favorite vegetables, no cook would be without favorite herbs growing close at hand. Fresh herbs can transform simple foods into gourmet delights. Their aromas and flavors add another dimension to most foods.

Every herb has its own personality and often takes the place of fat and salt to add extra flavor to cooked dishes. Each herb creates its own magic, but you need to remember that what goes well with one kind of food, such as chicken, may not taste the same when used with lamb or pork.

To test an herb, pick off a leaf and crush it in your hand. Its fragrance should be your guide. Parsley, chives, and dill impart a mild flavor. Basil, marjoram, oregano, rosemary, tarragon, thyme, and sage can easily overpower a dish. Experiment by combining these herbs and trying them in individual dishes.

For a dinner party, you can create centerpieces with small containers of different herbs bunched together. Drop mint sprigs in a glass of water and ice, or use them as napkin decorations by rolling the napkins and tying an herb sprig in place with a colorful bow.

Most cooks are familiar with a single variety of each herb. Actually there are many, and each one has a separate and distinct flavor. Fresh herbs bring out the flavor of poultry and seafood better than dried herbs. Dried herbs have a stronger flavor than fresh herbs, so if you use fresh herbs, use more than what you would with dried.

Even when you have no room for a kitchen garden, there's always a little extra space between the cracks for herbs. Grow herbs between stepping stones, along the sidewalk, or in the holes of a rock wall. The trick is to dig out a hole, fill it with potting mix, and plant it with your favorite herbs.

Chimney tiles, available from building supply stores, also make a good easy-care, easy-to-pick herb garden. With these tiles, it isn't necessary to kneel down to pick what you need. Fill them with planting mix, and plant the herb varieties of your choice. Use a drip system to make it easy to water. When the plants get woody, cut them back to initiate new growth.

What's In a Basket?

Some herbs do wonderfully well when grown in hanging baskets. They are decorative as well as space saving and can be hung under the eaves or from an outdoor post. Make sure, however, that they receive at least 6 hours of sunlight a day. Herb baskets also make great gifts for the gardening cook. Buy a small basket and fill it with thyme, parsley, oregano, and similar herbs you have started yourself or purchased from a nursery. You can even include herb growing tips if you like. Follow these steps:

1. Buy a 20-inch wire basket and a sack of thick sphagnum planting moss.
2. Thoroughly soak the moss and squeeze out the water.
3. Line the basket with moss, and add about 3 inches of potting mix.
4. Fill the basket with a good potting soil.
5. Plant the top and the sides with your choice of herbs.

To propagate herbs through cuttings or division, see Figures 4-2a through 4-2c.

The following ten herbs can be the mainstay of your herb garden. But don't stop with these—experiment and add more herbs to the garden as time goes on.

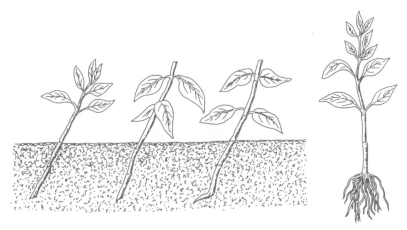

Figure 4-2. To propogate perennial herbs from cutting, cut at a slant below the growing node. Place your cutting in moist sand and move to a warm place. When you see new growth, transplant to a sunny window, then to individual containers.

Figure 4-2a. Dig up plant in the spring.

Figure 4-2b. Divide the roots into two separate plants

Figure 4-2c. Move both plants to a new location.

Basil

This aromatic herb is Karen's favorite, and she always has a separate herb bed for the various varieties she tries. She plants enough to dry plenty for winter use and uses the fresh basil well into fall. Basil comes in plenty of scents, colors, and sizes.

Dark Opal: Dark, purplish bronze leaves. Seed source: ABU COM COO DEG GAR GLE JOH LEJ LIB NIC ORG PAR PIN RIC SEE SHE SOU TAY VER WILL

Green Globe: Forms a dense globular little green bush with nice basil flavor. Excellent variety for pots or hanging baskets. Seed source: BURP COO RIC STO

Lemon: Compact bush with small, silver green leaves that have an intense lemon aroma. Excellent variety for fish. Seed source: ABU BURP COO DEG GAR GOU GUR HEN JOH LIB NIC PAR PIN POR RIC SEE SEED SHE SOU STO TAY TER VER WILL

Lettuce Leaf: 24-inch plant. 6-inch lettucelike crinkled leaves. Seed source: ABU COM DEG GAR GOU NIC PIN RIC SEE SEED SHE SOU STO TAY VER

Purple Ruffles: Clovelike aroma. Large heavily ruffled and fringed dark purple leaves. Seed source: ALL BURP COM COO DEG GOU JOH JUN LIB PAR PIN RIC SEE STO TAY TER TWI WILL

Sweet Basil: The most popular variety. Large, green, aromatic leaves. Seed source: ABU ALL BOU BURP BURR COM FIS GOU GUR HEN HIG JUN LED LIB ORG PAR POR RIC SEE SEED STO SUN TAY TER TWI VER WIL WILL

Chives

The round, hollow leaves have a delicate onion flavor that enhances cheese and egg dishes, gravies, and soups. Chives are usually purchased as small plants, but they can be grown from seed.

Curly Chives (*A. Senescens*): 8 inches tall. Flat leaves grow in a circular pattern. Seed source: DAB

Garden Chives (*A. Schoeno-prasum*): 1 foot tall. Leaves have mild onion flavor. Divide the clump every three years. Seed source: ABU ALL DAB BOU BURP BURR COM COO DEG FAR FIS GAR GOU GUR HEN HIG JOH LED LEJ LIB NIC PAR PIN POR RED RIC ROS SEE SHE SOU STO TAY TER TIL TWI VER WILL

Mauve Garlic Chives: Some great garlic flavor. Seed source: RIC

Schnittlauch: Thick tufts of dark green hollow foliage. Keep cut. Seed source: MEY

Dill

The seeds of dill have a sharp, slightly bitter taste that is reminiscent of caraway. Harvest the seeds when they are ripe and before they drop to the ground. Use the leaves fresh or dried. Seeds can also be used as a seasoning. For the greatest flavor, pick dill just as the flowers are opening.

Bouquet: Dwarf, compact plant that grows to 3 feet. Seed source: COM DEG FIS GLE JOH LEJ LIB ORN PAR RIC ROS SHE SOU TIL TWI VER

Dill (*A. Graveolens*): Finely cut foliage. 40-inch plant. Seed source: ABU ALL BOU BURP COM FAR GUR HEN HIG LED MEY NIC ORG PAR PIN POR RED RIC SEE SOU STO TAY WIL

Dukat: Has strong flavor and high oil content. Greener color than most dills. Seed source: COO GOU JOH ORN NIC PIN RIC SEED SHE TER

Fernleaf: 18-inch, dwarf plant. Dark green leaves. Seed source: BURP COM DEG GOU JOH JUN LIB NIC PAR PIN RIC SOU STO TER TWI VER WILL

Leaf: 40-inch plant. Bushy habit of dark green leaves. Slow to bolt. Seed source: RIC

Long Island Mammoth: Standard heirloom variety. Seed source: ABU COM DEG GAR JUN LEJ RIC SEED SOU VER WILL

Oregano

Oregano imparts a spicy, robust flavor to any recipe. There are several varieties you may want to try.

Greek: A strong-flavored oregano that grows to 6 feet. Slight licorice flavor. Seed source: ABU BOU DAB DEG GOU HIG LEJ ORN PAR PIN RIC SEE SEED SHE SOU TAY

Kalitera: Kalitera means "the best" in Greek. Spicy-scented, silver gray foliage. Seed source: RIC

Syran: A strong peppery flavor. The plant grows to 2 feet. Seed source: RIC

Turkestan: Strong flavor. Dark leaves. Seed source: RIC

Mint

There is probably no other herb that has more different tastes than that of mint. Flavors can resemble pineapple, apple, lemon, or ginger. Because mint tends to take over the garden, you might want to plant it in large pots sunk into the ground to keep its roots from spreading (Figure 4-3). Mint is good in mint sauce spread over vegetables; cooked with fish, lamb, and poultry; or used in jams and jellies.

Apple: Has fuzzy grayish leaves with apple fragrance. Seed source: DAB NIC RIC SHE TAY

Chocolate: Shiny, dark green leaves with a hint of chocolate scent. Grows 12 to 15 inches tall. Seed source: DAB NIC

Curly: Spearmint flavor. Seed source: DAB PAR

Ginger: Gold-flecked leaves have fruity fragrance and flavor of ginger. Grows 2 feet tall. Seed source: DAB RIC

Figure 4-3. Planting mint in large pots keeps roots from spreading.

Lemon: Soft, fuzzy foliage with lemon scent. Seed source: **COM DEG LEJ NIC PAR TAY VER**

Lime: Lime-scented mint. Seed source: **RIC**

Orange: Citrus fragrance, used in fruit punches and teas. 18-inch plant. Seed source: **DAB NIC RIC SHE TAY**

Pineapple: Wonderful aroma. Seed source: **DAB NIC RIC SHE TAY**

Marjoram

Marjoram is thought to have originated in the Orient. It complements the flavor of salads, vinegars, casseroles, stuffings, pork, chicken, and beef.

Annual Marjoram: Grows 16 inches tall. Much stronger flavor than Sweet Marjoram. Seed Source: **STO**

Sweet Marjoram: Grows 1 to 2 feet tall. Sweet oreganolike flavor. Seed source: **ABU BOU BURR COM COO DAB FIS GAR GOU HEN JOH LED LEJ LIB MEY NIC ORN PAR PIN POR RIC SEE SHE SOU STO TAY TER TIL TWI VER WIL WILL**

Parsley

Parsley is akin to carrots. It is a garnish for many dishes and is used as a flavoring for soups and stews. There are three main types: curled, plain leaved, and long rooted.

Curled Parsley

Emerald (Extra Curled Dwarf): Compact plant with dark green, finely cut and curled leaves. Seed source: **BURP NIC**

Evergreen (Double Curled): Deep green biennial plant that is frost resistant. Seed source: **ALL DAB BURR**

Forest Green: Dark green, densely curled, 15 inches high. Seed source: **GOU JOH LIB MEY ORG ORN SEED SOU TER TWI VER WIL**

Moss Curled: Also called Triple Curled. 12 inches high, and very dark green, closely curled. Seed source: **BURR COM DEG FIS HIG JUN LEJ MEY PIN ROS SEE SEED TIL VER WILL**

Plain-Leaved Parsley

Italian: Deeply cut, bright green leaves. Seed source: **ALL BURP**

BURR COM DEG FIS JOH LEJ LED LIB NIC RED SEE SHE SOU TIL TWI VER

Long-Rooted Parsley
Hamburg Long Rooted: 6 x 2 inches long. Parsniplike root is white. Seed source: BURP LED LIB MEY NIC PIN SEED TWI WILL

Rosemary

Rosemary is a hardy ever-green shrub. It grows 4 to 7 feet tall. We can hardly do anything without rosemary. Try it on southern fried chicken by sprinkling dried leaves on the pieces before you fry them. Rosemary sprigs beneath the skin of a roasting chicken or turkey will give the meat a delightful flavor. Just remove the sprigs after roasting, and throw them away.

Benden Blue: Upright growth, beautiful medium blue flowers, narrow leaves. Seed source: RIC

Majorca: Upright growth to trailing habit. Dark blue flowers. Seed source: RIC

Tarragon

Tarragon, with its subtle anise flavor, adds distinction to a sauce for chicken, fish, meat, and vegetables. French tarragon is an ancient herb known to the Greeks and Romans. It does not produce seed and can only be propagated from cuttings or root division. Buy it as plants.

Thyme

The strong, warm, clovelike flavor of thyme goes well in gumbos, bouillabaisse, and clam chowder. It goes well with onions, carrots, and beets. It uplifts stuffings for turkey and chicken. It flavors slow-cooking meat dishes.

Caraway: Delightful, sweet caraway scent and flavor. Seed source: RIC TAY

Coconut: Pleasant scent. Creeper variety. Seed source: RIC TAY

Creeping Lemon: Similar to wild thyme. Grows to about 8 inches thick and has a strong lemon scent. Seed source: RIC

English: Most popular variety, also called Common Thyme. Broad, dark green leaves. Seed source: ABU ALL BOU BURP COM DEG FIS GAR GOU HEN HIG JOH LEJ LIB NIC ORN PAR PIN RED RIC SEE SOU STO TAY TER TIL TWI VER WILL

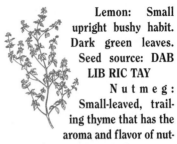

Lemon: Small upright bushy habit. Dark green leaves. Seed source: DAB LIB RIC TAY

Nutmeg: Small-leaved, trailing thyme that has the aroma and flavor of nutmeg. Seed source: DAB RIC

Chapter Five

The All-Inclusive Salad Garden

There is nothing like a big, bold, colorful salad to enhance meals. Salad lovers will want to grow varieties that include not only lettuce but also some unusual greens in colors ranging from green to magenta to chartreuse and in textures from smooth to curly. A kitchen gardener might want to plant radicchio, French dandelions, arugula, watercress, or curly endive among the various lettuces. And what a choice of lettuces are available, with names like Llolo Rosa, La Brilliante, Flame, Red Fire, Green Ice, and Salad Bowl. Add all shapes and colors of radishes, onions, tomatoes, and even edible flowers to the greens, and you've made an introduction to a meal.

A salad lover's kitchen garden should also contain different colored sweet peppers, cucumbers, celery, cauliflower, broccoli, and endive. A kitchen salad garden can be anything as simple as a couple of types of lettuce growing in a container on a patio or as elaborate as a raised-bed garden devoted entirely to salads. See Figures 5-1 to 5-4 for sample postage stamp kitchen salad gardens.

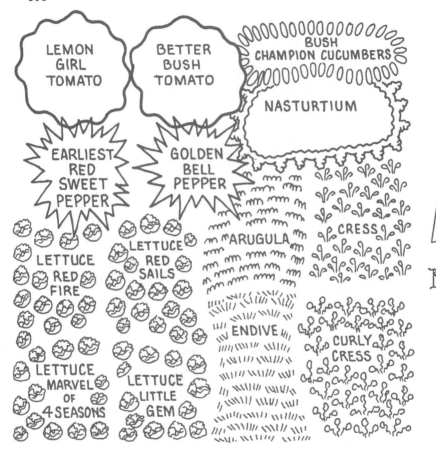

Figure 5-1. Small salad garden.

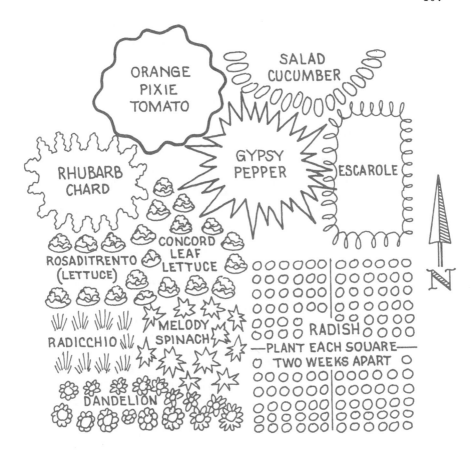

Figure 5-2. General salad garden.

Romaine Parris Island Cos / Little Gem Romaine	Romaine Parris Island Cos / Little Gem Romaine	Rouge D'Hiver Romaine / Little Gem Romaine	Rouge D'Hiver Romaine / Little Gem Romaine
Great Lakes Head Lettuce	Great Lakes Head Lettuce	Merveille Des Quatres Saisons Head Lettuce	Bibb Head Lettuce
Black Seeded Simpson Loose-Leaf Lettuce	Green Ice Loose-Leaf Lettuce	Salad Bowl Loose-Leaf Lettuce	Salad Bowl Red Loose Leaf
Lollo Rossa Loose-Leaf Lettuce / Oak Leaf Loose-Leaf Lettuce (Green)	Lollo Rossa Loose-Leaf Lettuce / Red Oak Leaf Lettuce	Red Sails Loose-Leaf Lettuce / Red Oak Leaf Lettuce	Red Sails Loose-Leaf Lettuce / Oak Leaf Loose-Leaf Lettuce (Green)

Figure 5-3. Lettuce bed. 4' x 4' bed.

Batavian Full Hearted Escarole	Tres Fine Maraichere Endive	Givlio (Radicchio)	Givlio (Radicchio)
Lettuce Red Sails	Majestic Red Lettuce Romaine	Jerico Romaine Lettuce	Buttercrunch Bibb Lettuce
Upland Cress	Garden Cress	Arugula	Tennis Ball Buttercrunch Lettuce
Montmagny Dandelion	Melody Spinach	Susan's Red Bibb Lettuce	Green Tea Lettuce

Figure 5-4. Small green bed. 4' x 4' bed.

There's a revolution going on today in the salad bowl. Salad lovers have so many greens at their fingertips that it's hard to know where to start. Prepackaged salad mixes are showing up at supermarkets all across the United States. They are beautiful and tempting, but will never be as fresh as those from your own garden. Karen checks out the packages that look good to her and then duplicates the ingredients in our garden.

Don't be afraid to try different combinations of greens with lettuces. Mix in chicory, mustard, kale, Swiss chard, purslane, chervil (both a green and an herb), and even edible flowers such as bachelor's buttons, calendulas, pansies, or nasturtiums. Even a small kitchen garden will let you grow a number of different greens, making it easy to toss together a variety of colors, textures, and flavors that will spice up any salad. Most greens grow quickly and are ready to harvest in 6 to 12 weeks. The following section offers a quick tour of what you can grow in a kitchen salad garden.

Greens

Here are some salad green basics:

- Pick fresh crisp leaves.
- Wash them in a colander under slightly warm running water as soon as you pick them.
- Remove any wilted or bruised spots. Rinse them in cold water.
- Put the greens in a wire basket, and shake them to remove all water.
- Place the greens in a plastic bag along with a paper towel to remove the remaining moisture.

Greens that Thrive in Hot Weather

Many greens are cool-weather vegetables that struggle in hot summer weather. In our area, we can only grow them successfully in fall and spring. There are a few greens, however, that grow well in warm weather, so you can enjoy fresh salads all summer long.

Amaranth: Tasty, tall, ornamental plant that grows 3 feet high. Plant the edible leaf varieties. Seed source: COO ORN SEE SEED

Malabar Spinach: A trailing vine that grows well up a trellis. The leaves taste much like spinach. Seed source: COO ORN SEE SEEO

Orach: Also called Mountain Spinach. Comes in different colors. Tastes like spinach. Keep the end leaves pinched back. Seed source: COO ORN SEE SEED

Arugula

Sometimes called rocket, arugula has dark green leaves that are peppery pungent. We planted arugula several years ago and were surprised to find that it lasts the entire year, reseeds itself nicely, and spreads everywhere. For more zip, combine this with sweet or bitter greens such as mustard.

Seed source: GUR NIC RED

Chard

Chard has huge leaves and crisp stems and is one of the easiest greens to grow. The stems have a celerylike taste and texture, and the leaves have a flavor that's stronger than spinach. The varieties that you can grow at home are sweeter than the ones you find in the market. Chard can be grown most of the year and has red or green, crumpled or smooth leaves.

Erbette: Smooth green leaves that make a great cut-and-come-again plant. Seed source: COO

Fordhook Giant: Dark green, crumpled leaves have snow-white midribs. Seed source: ABU ALL BURP COM FIS GAR HIG JOH MEY ORN PON RED ROS SEE STO TER TWI VER WIL

Lucullus: Large, white midribs, light green crumpled leaves. Seed

source: ABU ALL FAR GUR HEN JUN LED PAR SEE TIL VER WILL

Rhubarb Chard: Crimson stalks with heavily crumpled green leaves. Seed source: ABU ALL BURP BURR COM DEG FAR FIS GAR JOH LED NIC ORG ORN PIN SEE SEED SHE STO TER TIL TWI VER WILL

Cress

All of the "cresses" listed here, although not in the same family, have the same peppery-sharp taste. All the cresses will add an extra sharp flavor to avocado salad, five-bean salad, or almost any other salad.

Garden Cress: Finely curled parsleylike leaves. It's an annual, reaching maturity in about 35 days. Seed source: ABU ALL COM DEG FIS LEJ JOH JUN KIT NIC SEE SEED SHE STO TOM WIL

Upland Cress: Not actually a cress, but is similar to watercress. It has broad bright green leaves and dense growth. Grows in any type of soil. Seed source: ABU BURP COM DEG JLH NIC RIC SEE SOU TAY VER

Watercress: This peppery-flavored green is a member of the nasturtium family and is often blended with lettuces for salads. Refrigerate watercress with its stems in a cup of water to keep it fresh. Watercress has small oval leaves and likes to grow near water or very moist soil. Seed source: RIC SOU

Dandelion

Dandelion is a bitter green. The leaves of the variety used in salads are elongated. They are not the dandelions growing in your lawn.

Montmagny: This is a thick-leaved, full-hearted dandelion. It can be used in a soup, salad, or stir-fry. Seed source: LEJ

Thick-Leaved: Has bitter broad leaves. Seed source: BURP STO

Endive

This particular plant can be confusing because it's classified as chicory, which includes radicchio, endive curled, and endive not curled, along with cutting chicory. Confusing!

Let's try to clarify some of the confusion here. All three can be used in salads calling for lettuce. Don't use endive in place of lettuce, but combine the two—Belgian endive, curly endive, escarole, frisee, and radicchio all have a sharp, jolting taste that adds a tongue-tingling sensation to any salad. They are definitely an acquired taste.

Cutting Chicory

Spadona: Also called Dog's Tongue, has smooth leaves that should be cut when 4 to 6 inches tall. Seed source: COO

Endive (Not Curled)

Batavian Full Hearted: Slightly crumpled, dark green leaves with a 12-inch spread. White rib and tender heart. Also called Escarole. Seed source: BOU GAR LED PIN STO TIL TWI

Endive (Curled)

Use it for its coarse frilly leaves and tart taste.

Tres Fine Maraichere: A French variety with green, frilly outer leaves. Crunchy white ribs. Seed source: GOU HIG SHE

Radicchio (Semiheading and Heading)

You can pick the outer leaves for the flavor and color.

Giulio: Full-sized head, deep burgundy with white veins. Looks like a tiny red cabbage and is the type you'd find in supermarkets. Bitter and beautiful in salads. Seed source: COO HIG JOH NIC ORN SHE

Witloof Chicory: The forcing variety, with 4- to 6-inch-long white heads. Also known as Belgian Endive, this variety is found in supermarkets and mostly used as a stuffed appetizer. Seed source: COM HIG LED PIN RED SEE WILL

Kale

There are two kinds of kale: smooth leaved and curly. The curly kales have compact clusters of tightly curled leaves. The smooth-leaved type has coarse, but smooth leaves. Some varieties find their way into salads, either raw or slightly cooked.

Dwarf Blue Curled Vates: Leaves are finely curled and bluish green. A low compact, short-stemmed plant. Seed source: ABU BURP BUT COM DEG GAR GUR HEN JUN LED LIB MEY NIC ROS SEE SOU STO TIL TWI WIL

Russian Red: Wavy, red purple leaves. 2-foot-tall plant. Seed source: ABU BOU GAR JLH JOH NIC ORG ORN PIN SEED SHE SOU

Lettuce

We covered some lettuce varieties in the previous chapter, but there are so many good varieties that we'd like to give you even more choices to try. In our garden, we always have a spring and fall lettuce bed with many varieties to choose from. When spring turns to tomato planting season, we plant lettuce in this bed so that the tomatoes will provide shade and the lettuce will continue growing longer than it usually would. We also plant lettuce in clay pots, barrels, hanging baskets, or other creative containers for our patio, which is beneath a canopy of oak trees and provides a cool place for them to grow. Our patio is just steps from the kitchen and certainly qualifies as a kitchen garden. One trick for summer lettuce is to water it heavily to avoid bitterness.

Here are some general tips for using lettuce:

- A pound of leaf lettuce or romaine produces 6 cups of torn pieces. A pound of endive produces about 4 cups.
- Greens last longer if you wash them as soon as you pick them.
- To keep greens perky, not wilted, wash, dry, and wrap them in a dish towel, and then refrigerate them until you're ready to make your salad.
- Clean tight heads of lettuce by tapping the firm end of the head against the counter, then twist the core out. Clean by rinsing with the core end up. Make sure water gets in between the leaves.

Head Lettuce

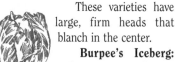

These varieties have large, firm heads that blanch in the center.

Burpee's Iceberg: Light green, wavy leaves. Seed source: BURP

Deer Tongue: A medium-sized butterhead type. Triangular, green leaves with rounded tips. Seed source: ABU GAR SHE

Reine Des Glaces: Also known as Ice Queen, has deeply cut, lacy, green leaves. Seed source: COO ORN SEE

Susan's Red Bibb: Ruffled leaves have rose margins. Seed source: SOU

Romaine Lettuce

This lettuce is sometimes called cos, and has tall, loose leaves that form a head.

Jericho: An Israeli variety with sword-shaped leaves. It is adapted to many climates. Seed source: SHE

Majestic Red: Tall, green leaves overlaid with deep burgundy. This is a loose-leaf romaine. Seed source: TER WILL

Parris Island Cos: 8- to 9-inch-tall head. Dark green leaves. Seed source: BURP COM GAR HEN JOH LIB MEY PIN POR RED SEE SEED SOU STO TIL VER WIL WILL

Loose-Leaf Lettuce

Loose leaf is a fast-growing lettuce. It's called the cut-and-come-again vegetable because the more leaves you remove, the faster it seems to grow.

Corcarde: Trumpet-shaped head with lobed, dark green leaves with rusty red hues. This is an oak leaf type. Seed source: JOH SEED

Green Ice: Has savoyed, dark green leaves with fringed margins. Seed source: ALL BURP COM COO JUN LED ORN PAR PIN PON

Red Fire: Savoyed and frilled, intensely red leaves. Seed source: GAR JOH LIB PIN STO VER

Red Sails: Another prize, heavily ruffled, deep red bronze leaves. Seed source: ALL BOU BURR COM COO DEG GUR HEN JUN LIB MEY NIC ORN PAR PIN POR SOU STO TER TIL TWI VER WILL

Rossa D'Amerique: Italian cutting lettuce has pale green leaves tipped with sparkling rose red. Seed source: COO

Rossa Di Trento: Another Italian cutting lettuce. Has savoyed green leaves with wine red margins. Seed source: COO

Mustard

Very few gardeners know how good mustard greens taste in salads. Tender young mustard leaves have a peppery nip and a mild, distinctive taste appreciated by almost all adventurous eaters. Substitute chopped mustard greens for half the lettuce in salads.

Three kinds of mustard greens are usually available: smooth leaf, curly leaf, and oriental. The curly leaved types are superior for salads. They seem to fluff up tossed salads, much like curly endive. We always grow oriental mustard in our spring and fall garden for a stir-fry. We also use the tender leaves in salads.

Curled Mustard

Southern Giant Curled: Plant spreads 18 to 24 inches. Wide, crumpled bright green leaves. Seed source: BOU BURR DEG JUN LED MEY PAR POR ROS SEE SUN TIL TWI WIL

Plain Mustard

Savannah: Smooth, thick, dark green leaves with narrow, cream-colored ribs. This is a large plant. Seed source: LED PAR TWI VER

Oriental Mustard (Green Stalks)

Chinese Tsi Shim: Light green leaves and flowering stalks. Harvest when the flowers begin to open. Seed source: GAR SUN

Mei Quing Choi: A vase-shaped plant with pale green stems and oval, green leaves. Seed source: BOU DEG JOH NIC ORN PAR PIN SHE STO TWI VER

Oriental Mustard (White Stalks, Spoon-Shaped Leaves)

Bok Choi: Also called Bok Choy. Thick, green leaves and broad, white stalks. Seed source: GUR HEN LIB NIC SEED STO SUN THE

Mitsuba: Plain, parsleylike leaves on long, slender white stems. Seed source: GLE VER

Sorrel

This is a relative newcomer as a garden green. It has narrow-shaped leaves with a crisp, yet tender, texture and a sharp lemonlike tang. **Seed source: BURP**

Spinach

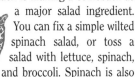

Spinach is making a comeback as a major salad ingredient. You can fix a simple wilted spinach salad, or toss a salad with lettuce, spinach, and broccoli. Spinach is also used for a filling that goes into lasagna or quiche.

Savoyed

Bloomsdale Long Standing: Very crinkled, glossy, dark green leaves. Seed source: ABU ALL BURP BURR BUT DEG FAR GAR GUR HEN HIG JLH JUN LED LIB MEY NIC PAR PIN PLA RED SEE SOU STO TIL VER WIL WILL

Semisavoyed

Melody: Has dark green leaves. Seed source: BURP FAR GOU HEN JUN LED MEY NIC PAR PIN POR STO TWI VER

Smooth-Leaved

Nobel Giant: Huge, thick, smooth, pointed green leaves with round tips. Seed source: BURR DEG HEN JLH SEE TIL

Spinach Substitutes

Use these just like you would spinach.

New Zealand Spinach: Small, brittle, triangular-shaped green leaves. Plant spreads across the bed. Seed source: ALL BOU BURP BUT COM DEG FAR GAR GOU HEN JLH JUN LED LIB MEY NIC PIN POR RED ROS SEE SOU STO VER WILL

Orach, Green: Will grow to 6 feet if not cut. Seed source: BOU PIN

Orach, Red: Annual, red purple variety. Seed source: COO NIC PIN SEE

Tampala Spinach: Tastes like an artichoke. Seed source: BURG POR SEE

Mesclun

Mesclun is a mixture of young salad greens grown in the same bed. This is the French approach to salad greens, and one that Americans are catching on to. They are usually cool-weather greens, sown to be harvested in spring or early fall. Plant four lettuce varieties, head and loose leaf in red and green. This creates color and texture. Then add arugula and radicchio for spice and a touch of bitterness. These will be tempered by the sweeter greens. Add mustards that range from mild to sharp. Remember that baby greens are naturally milder than the more mature ones. You can sprinkle in herbs such as chervil, chives, onion, and edible flowers—and this is your mesclun garden.

If you are mixing your own mesclun, just dump all the seeds in a bowl and stir. Then broadcast the seed as evenly as you can over a bed of loose, rich soil. Settle them with a rake, then water. When the greens are 4 to 6 inches high, snip them with scissors about an inch above the ground. Wash the greens, dry them, and then toss them into a salad bowl.

Tomatoes

Because there are literally thousands of varieties of vegetables to choose from, we try not to repeat from chapter to chapter, and tomatoes are no exception. Because tomatoes are an absolute for salads, we want to give you some varieties that will show off your salads or bring something special to them. Let your imagination go wild when it comes time to think about tomatoes.

Pink Tomatoes

Pink Girl: Indeterminate pink, 8-ounce, globe-shaped tomato. Seed source: GUR HEN LIB PAR PON TOM TOMA

Tennessee Peach Fuzz: 2 inches in diameter, dark pink, unusual skin texture. Seed source: SEE

Orange/Yellow/Gold Tomatoes

Brandywine Yellow: Indeterminate yellow version of the pink variety. Seed source: SEE TOM TOMA

Golden Boy: Indeterminate plant. Large, deep yellow globe fruit. Seed source: COM LEJ PIN TOM TOMA VER WIL

Lemon Boy: Our favorite yellow tomato. Indeterminate plant. Bright lemon yellow, 8 to 10 ounces. Seed source: BURP DEG HEN JLH LIB NIC PAR POR STO TER TOM TOMA VER WILL

Small-Fruited Tomatoes

Cherry Grande VF: Determinate plant. $1^1/_2$-inch red fruit. Seed source: STO TOM TOMA TWI

Gardener's Delight: Indeterminate. Bite-sized, $1/_2$- to $3/_4$-inch red tomatoes. Seed source: BOU BURP COO GAR PAR PIN SEE SEED THO TOM TOMA

Orange Pixie: Determinate plant has orange, $1^1/_2$-inch fruit. Seed source: TOM

Pink Pear: Indeterminate plant. Tiny pink pear-shaped tomatoes. Seed source: TOM

Red Currant: Indeterminate plant with tiny red fruit. Spread a cloth beneath the plant, and shake to harvest. Seed source: COO DEG JLH JOH SEED TOM

Red Pear: Indeterminate. Clusters of 1-inch red fruit. Seed source: BURG COO DEG GLE HEN JOH ORN SEE STO TOM

Sun Gold: Indeterminate. Bite-sized, bright tangerine color. Seed source: JOH TER THO TOMA

Sweet 100: Our favorite small variety, it lasts an entire season with plenty to give away. Indeterminate plant with red, cherry-sized tomatoes that grow in clusters. Seed source: BURP COM COO GUR HEN LIB MEY ORN POR SHE STO THO TIL TOM TOMA TWI

Yellow Currant: Indeterminate. Yellow currant-sized tomatoes. Seed source: COO GLE JOH NIC TOM TOMA

Yellow Pear: Indeterminate. Clusters of $1^1/_4$-by-2-inch yellow pear-shaped fruit. Seed source: ABU ALL BURP COO DEG GAR GLE GOU HEN HIG JOH MEY NIC ORN POR SEE SEED SHE SOU STO TOM TOMA WIL WILL

The Creative Salad Palette

Salads, of course, are a lot more than just pretty greens, and as already indicated, you can include almost any vegetable on your salad palette. Adding colored sweet peppers, cucumbers, tomatoes, and beans is a good start. Then include carrots, peas, corn, and a touch of herbs. You can also include fruit in any vegetable salad. Try adding melon balls and cucumbers, topped with a cucumber mint dressing. A crunchy chicken salad could be mixed with apple, spinach, and broccoli. Or try crab with wild rice, including celery, red pepper, and fresh snap or snow peas. You can add shrimp and prosciutto to dress up any salad, and if there are enough greens, color, and texture, the salad could be a main meal.

Want a tangy salad that makes your taste buds sit up and take notice? Try this one. Mix 2 cups of fresh basil leaves with about 8 cups of leaf lettuce. Combine with 3 tablespoons of vinegar and 2 teaspoons of olive oil.

Celeriac (celery root) doesn't exactly spring to mind when you say salad, but it can actually be the mainstay of a number of tasty salads, such as Waldorf salad. Celeriac is the exact opposite of celery. Celery is grown for its stalks and, sometimes, its leaves; celeriac is grown for its tuber, which has the crunchiness of celery with the texture of a turnip. Cook the tuber in boiling water until tender, cool, cut into cubes, and combine in your salad.

If you are looking for a different vegetable to add to your salad, try fennel. It comes in two forms: green and bronze. The seeds are used in baking; the leaves are used for flavor or for decoration in fish and egg dishes. To use in a salad, cut off and discard any woody stems. Cut off the feathery leaves, but save them. Mix both head and leaves with other ingredients, such as lettuce and onions. Fennel salad is good served hot or cold.

Sweet Fennel: Smokey bronze leaves. Seed source: EOR PAR

Smokey Fennel: Large fleshy variety, distinctive flavor. Seed source: ABU

Florence Fennel: Copper tinged foliage. Seed source: ABU COM NIC PIN RED SEE SHE SOU TAX

Finally, are you trying to find a gift for a good cook? Why not give a salad garden? A salad garden, for instance, might include a decorative pot, gloves, soil, and seed packages of salad greens such as arugula, butterhead lettuce, curly endive, escarole, and several varieties of loose-leaf lettuce.

Chapter Six

The Vegetarian and Cooking Light Garden

Vegetarian and low-fat cooking is exploding across the nation, with cooks everywhere striving to serve good-tasting, nutritious meals with home-grown vegetables. Carole Peck, a California master chef, stresses combining imagination, a clear vision, and the freshest carefully chosen ingredients.

Many kitchen gardeners who are not vegetarian still enjoy meatless meals. It's easy to start with just a few vegetables, using herbs and spices in such favorites as stuffed baked potatoes or crusty vegetable pie.

Start with the basic vegetable list from Chapter 4 and two 4-by-4-foot beds for the first year, then expand the beds as you gain experience or want to try new vegetables. Again, we urge you to keep a notebook. Record what varieties you grow, what recipes you use them in, and what flavors you enjoy the most.

See Figures 6-1 and 6-2 for an array of gardens designed for vegetarian cooks. The emphasis is on those vegetables you will use the most. We like tomatoes in the summer, along with squash and peppers. In our winter garden, we like oriental cabbage, snow peas, broccoli, and other winter vegetables.

124

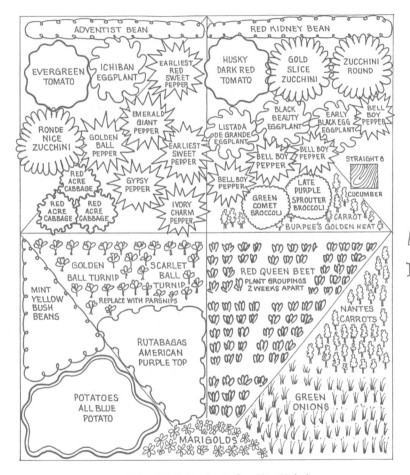

Figure 6-1. Vegetarian garden. 10' x 10' bed.

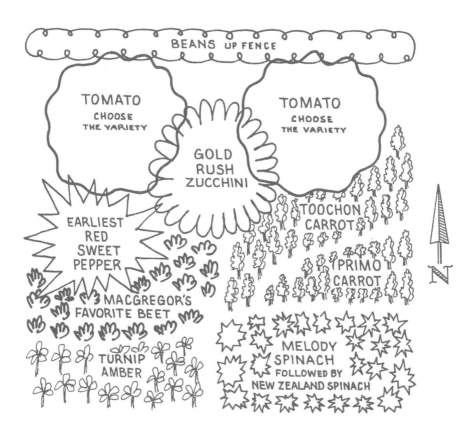

Figure 6-2. Vegetarian garden. 4' x 4' bed.

Vegetarians who are particular about taste should select their varieties with care since almost every vegetable variety has a slightly different flavor. We suggest you start with some of the varieties listed here. Then, add to your selection as you gain confidence in your garden. Some gardening cooks become so interested with this that they wind up growing dozens of varieties of the same vegetable. We know of gardeners who have grown as many as 300 bean varieties over the last ten years. One word of warning: once you get started it could well become a lifelong journey.

Shell Beans

Beans are a tremendous protein source (instead of meat) used by most vegetarians. There are literally hundreds of bean varieties to choose from, yet only a handful of cooks grow more than two or three varieties. Good chefs use as many different varieties as possible for texture, flavor, and color. The beans' earthy flavor and starchy texture marry well with other foods. Innovative recipes include black bean cakes with greens and apple dressing, bean spaghetti, and black bean terrine with fresh tomatoes and jalapeño sauce.

Here are some varieties you might like to try.

Adventist: Small, golden bean used in soups and stews. Seed source: ORG

Beautiful: Creamy white bean with a maroon design that looks as if it's painted on. This bean is easy to digest since it produces little gas. Seed source: GAR

Cannellini: An Italian, dry, kidney-shaped white bean. Seed source: PIN

Cliff Dweller: An ancient Southwest heirloom bean that is heat and drought resistant. Seed source: SOU

Cluster Bean Barasati: This bean is used in East Indian cooking. Seed source: JLH

Hutterite Soup: An 1760s heirloom bean that makes a thick, creamy soup. Seed source: SEED

Lentil Masoor: A tiny, dark skinned, salmon orange interior seed that cooks rather quickly. Seed source: JLH

Moth Bean: In India, the young pods are eaten as a vegetable. The high-protein dried beans are used like lentils. Seed source: BOU JLH

Sonoran Tepary Bean: This small gold bean is 30 percent crude protein. It is a native to the Sonoran Desert. Seed source: PLA RED SEED

Urdi Black: Popular in India, this small black bean is used in soups and sauces and even ground into meal. Seed source: JLH

Vermont Cranberry Pole: Tastes like steak. An heirloom soup bean with the same characteristics as the Vermont Cranberry bush. Seed source: ABU VER

Root Vegetables

The overlooked root vegetables such as parsnips, turnips, and rutabaga and salsify as well as beets and carrots, add a healthy change of pace to a vegetarian and low-fat diet.

Beets and carrots can be grown together in a large container. We also suggest putting all your root vegetables together in a 4-by-4-foot bed. In milder climates you can harvest these vegetables all year.

Root vegetables are usually grown during spring, fall and winter months (in warm winter areas), but most store well and can be used at any time. Here are some root varieties to choose from.

Beets

Beets are one of the sweetest vegetables you can grow. In most areas you can grow them summer, spring, and fall. Beets come in red, white, gold, and a combination of red and white.

Golden Beet: A good pickler. Its golden color won't bleed. Seed source: ABU BURP COO FIS GLE GUR HIG JUN LED NIC ORN PIN PON SEE SHE STO SOU WILL

Macgregor's Favorite: This Scottish variety has 3-inch elongated roots. Seed source: COO GAR ORN

Pacemaker III: This blood red beet is globe shaped and has a sweet flavor. Seed source: POR STO TWI

Ruby Queen: Dark red, somewhat elongated root. Seed source: BURR COM DEG FAR GUR HEN JUN LED MEY PAR PIN PON RED SEE STO TWI VER WIL

Carrots

Carrots are a vegetarian's favorite, and one of the most nutritious vegetables in your garden. They supply Vitamin B, B_2, and C, and are especially rich in Vitamin A. Vegetarians love carrots for their fiber content. Try creamy carrots with horseradish, Sugar Snap peas and carrots, or orange-fennel carrots.

Burpee's Goldinheart: $5^1/_2$ by $2^1/_4$ inches. Seed source: BURP

Primo: This French variety has no green shoulder and can also be picked and used as a baby carrot. Seed source: HIG

Touchon: Red orange, 7-by-1$\frac{1}{2}$-inch carrot of excellent quality. Seed source: ABU COO DEG FAR GUR HEN HIG LEJ NIC SEE STO

Celeriac

Known as celery root, this vegetable is knobby, hairy and brown. It has a crunchy, creamy white flesh and mild flavor.

Brillant: Medium large roots, white interior. Seed source: JOH TER

Prague: Large roots. Seed source: SEE

Leeks

Leeks do not bulb as onions do, but have thickened white skins. The green leaves on top should be thick and wrapped tightly around each other. Blanch by hilling the soil around them.

King Richard: 12-inch tall shaft, light green leaves. Seed source: COO FIS CAG GUR HIG JOH PIN

Splendid: Danish variety. Seed source: STO TER

Parsnips

You can exchange french fries for fried parsnips. Combine dried breadcrumbs, salt, and pepper. Cook $\frac{3}{4}$ pound of parsnips in boiling water for about 20 minutes or until tender. Cut cooled parsnips into strips and coat them with the breadcrumb mixture. Add to hot oil for about 1 minute, then drain. Try also a parsnip and carrot medley, a turnip and carrot stir-fry, or beet fritters.

Hollow Crown: 12-by-2$\frac{3}{4}$-inch 1850 heirloom parsnip. Smooth, white roots. Seed source: ABU ALL BURP BURR BUT COM DEG FAR PAR SEE SEED SOU VER

Jung's White Sugar: White skin, stocky, heavy at the shoulders. Seed source: JUN

Rutabagas

Rutabagas resemble turnips, but have deep yellow flesh and are sweeter. Rutabagas are good storers.

American Purple Top: Purple-topped, buttery yellow, 4- to 6-inch globe. Good winter storage. Heirloom variety. Seed source: **ALL BURR DEG FIS GUR HEN JUN LIB MEY PAR PON POR SEE SOU TIL TWI VER**

Laurentian Neckless: Purple top, yellow globe. Seed source: **ABU FAR GAR LIB PIN SEE STO WILL**

Salsify

Also called the oyster plant, it has long, thin, black roots with white flesh. It is good both raw with dips and cooked with a strong sauce.

Long Black: Long, black, very hardy. Seed source: **NIC SEF THE**

White French: White root, good oyster flavor. Seed source: **TIL**

Turnips

Turnips, cut into slices or strips, make a nice addition to any relish tray. Cooked turnips can be a side dish, and diced turnips can be added to soups and stews. Try using turnips in a coleslaw, or scalloped potatoes and turnips.

Amber: Yellowish globe with yellow flesh, 6-inch turnip. Seed source: **MEY POR SEE**

De Milan: This white globed, 2-by-4-inch turnip can be used as a baby beet. Tops are rosy red. French variety. Seed source: **GOU PIN SEE SHE**

Golden Ball: 4 inches across, round, yellow-fleshed heirloom variety. Seed source: **ABU BOU GLE JLH NIC ORN WILL**

Scarlet Ball: Slightly flattened, deep scarlet, semiglobe turnip with white flesh. Looks much like a beet. Seed source: **GLE NIC**

Tokyo Cross: White globe, 6 inches across. Seed source: **BURP FIS GUR HEN JUN MEY PIN POR TWI VER WILL**

White Lady: $2^1/_2$ inches, pure white, egg-shaped turnip. Seed source: **ORN PAR POR STO TWI**

Vegetarian Specialties

Vegetarian cuisine need no longer be humble. Innovative chefs nationwide have accepted vegetarian cooking into the world of sophisticated dining. This includes herbed sweet-and-sour onions with red peppers, broccoli with lemon cream, spicy stir-fried broccoli, Italian stuffed artichokes, and much more.

Here are a few more special varieties you'll want in your vegetarian garden.

Artichoke

Imperial Star: Tender, sweet, meat and nutty-tasting hearts. Seed source: SHE

Broccoli

Mercedes: This is the broccoli for vegetarians who don't like the strong broccoli flavor of most varieties. It can be eaten raw. Seed source: SHE

Onion

Early Ativa: The earliest miniature onion available. It has a flattened shape and a silvery white color. You can bake or boil them or serve them with other vegetables such as carrots or peas in a cream sauce. Seed source: SHE

Red Florence: A long, spindle-shaped onion, mild flavor. Seed source: COO

Peppers

Giant Yellow Banana: Sweet, bright yellow. Seed source: STO

Quadrato D'Oro: A Dutch introduction. It has large, golden fruit and a sweet flavor. Seed source: SHE

Rampage: Good flavor, thick walls, bright red. Seed source: PIN TOMA

Grilled Vegetables

Grilled vegetables are our favorite way to prepare summer vegetables. Slice zucchini, golden straightneck or crookneck squash, eggplant, and red peppers, coat them with a fine olive oil and herbs such as basil, and cook them directly on the grill. The flavors become more intense, and the crisp surface seals in the rich, smoky goodness. Cooks also use corn, tomatoes, onions, and a variety of other summer vegetables for the grill. If you spray a cold grill with olive oil or shortening, the vegetables won't stick. Or if you prefer, you can put the sliced vegetables in aluminum foil and cook until tender.

Here are some of our favorite varieties for the grill.

Eggplant

Asian Bride: 7 inches long, white skin, streaked lavender. Seed source: COO SHE

Ichiban: 12 inches long, purple. Seed source: BURR COM DEG GUR LE PAR PIN POR TWI VER

Listada De Gandia: 10 inches long, white with purple stripes. An Italian heirloom variety. Seed source: ORN SEE SEED SOU

Zucchini

Black Magic: Glossy, black green. Seed source: GUR HEN JUN VER

Gold Rush: A glossy, golden zucchini. Beautiful grilled. Seed source: BURR COM DEG GOU GUR JOH JUN LED LIB MEY NIC ORN PIN PON POR ROS STO TER TIL VER WIL WILL

Ronde De Nice: A 6-inch, round, pale green zucchini. When cut, oiled, and herbed, it looks, smells, and tastes great. Seed source: BOU GOU SEED SHE

Sweet Pepper

Earliest Red Sweet: 3 by 4 inches, bright red. Seed source: HIG PIN STO

Corn

Illinichief Xtra Sweet: Yellow extra-sweet corn. Seed source: POR

Squash

Crookneck Squash

Sundance: Bright yellow skin, creamy white inside. Seed source: BURG COM LIB NIC PIN STO VER WIL

Straightneck Squash

Butterstick: Golden yellow, white fleshed. We pick this one when it's fairly small. Seed source: BURP TER

Wrap and Bake or Grill

Another great way to make vegetables fun is to wrap them in parchment, aluminum foil, phyllo, or even leafy greens. Start with a 13-by-12-inch sheet of your wrap of choice, fold it in half crosswise, draw half a heart shape on the wrap, and cut along the drawn line. Open and place the wrap flat on a counter, and spray the wrap with nonstick coating. Combine in a bowl zucchini, yellow squash, sweet pepper, rings of onion, and basil. Then place green beans onto the square, and put the vegetables from the bowl onto the beans. Turn the edges of the square over, and seal by twisting the ends. Bake in a 400°F oven for about ten minutes.

An alternative is to wrap vegetables in foil and put them on the grill. Try asparagus spears, Italian green beans, summer or winter squash, potatoes, corn on the cob, or even carrots. Set the package 4 to 6 inches over medium coals. Cook 15 to 20 minutes, turning to cook evenly. Be inventive with your selection of vegetables, and try anything that looks good.

Vegetarian Side Dishes

Kitchen gardeners often create tantalizing side dishes to add to a more complicated vegetarian or light menu. These side dishes can complement, rather than compete with, the entree. For lemony cucumbers, score 2 cucumbers and combine them with $1/4$ cup vinegar, 2 tablespoon sugar, 2 tablespoons chopped onion, 1 tablespoon lemon juice, and 1 teaspoon celery seeds. Cover and chill 4 hours and serve. Any variety of cucumber will do, but here's one we recommend.

Burpless Hybrid: A 10-inch-long nonbitter cucumber. Seed source:	**BURP DEG FAR FIS LED LEJ PIN PON POR TIL**

Another side dish might be mint-glazed baby carrots. Steam 8 baby carrots. Melt 3 tablespoons of margarine or butter in a large skillet; stir in 2 tablespoons of sugar and 2 tablespoons of finely chopped fresh mint. Add carrots and cook 8 minutes. Stir well to glaze. Garnish with fresh mint sprigs. Here's one variety we recommend.

Baby Spike: A 3-by-$1/2$-inch orange carrot. Seed source: GUR HEN PAR POR	

Pizza for Vegetable Lovers

A low-calorie, healthy pizza is a dieter's dream. You can, of course, buy vegetarian pizza, but it will never taste as good as when it's made from your own garden-fresh vegetables. Make or buy the pizza crust, and make or buy the sauce. What really makes this pizza special is the fresh vegetables you'll put on top. We suggest onions, garlic, zucchini, sweet red and yellow peppers, eggplant, asparagus, artichokes, olives, and mushrooms. Of course the olives, mushrooms, and artichokes can be purchased at the market if you aren't lucky enough to actually be able to grow these ingredients.

Chop the onion and garlic (in a processor if you prefer). Add a cup of Italian tomato sauce, basil, and oregano. Spread half this sauce over a crust and set aside the rest. Slice the zucchini, mushrooms, artichoke, and olives over half the pizza. Slice the red and yellow peppers and eggplant over the other half of the pizza. Sprinkle mozzarella and Parmesan cheese over the entire pizza. Repeat the vegetable layering, then bake according to the crust you've selected. See Figure 6-3 for a specialty pizza garden.

Any variety of onion, garlic, and zucchini will do. We suggest that you try these peppers and eggplant.

Long Sweet Banana: A sweet pepper that turns from yellow to red when fully ripe. Seed source: ABU BURP COM DEG GUR HEN JUN LIB MEY NIC ORN PAR PIN PON POR ROS SOU STO TOMA TWI VER WIL WILL

Cardinal: A large, blocky red pepper. Seed source: STO

Short Tom: A long Japanese eggplant that makes convenient-sized slices when cut up. Seed source: TER

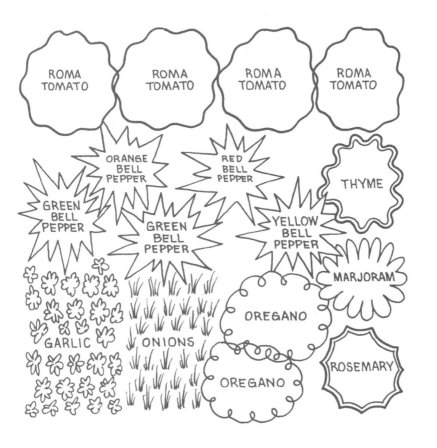

Figure 6-3. Pizza garden. 4' x 4' bed.

Chapter Seven

The Italian Kitchen Garden

No where is the connection between garden and plate more clearly drawn than in Italy. In summer, there are open-air markets everywhere. Tables are mounded with red, green, orange, and yellow sweet peppers, the ripest tomatoes, the greenest zucchini, and piles of Romano beans. Everyone recognizes the taste of a good Italian tomato sauce and the use of fresh basil over fresh pasta. Italian cooks not only use a lot of daily pasta with light sauces but also are clever in the use of beans, broccoli, eggplant, artichokes, radicchio, greens, and many other vegetables.

Inspired Italian cooks stress vegetables in zucchini antipasto dishes, a wide variety of cortoni (vegetable dishes served at room temperature or gently warmed), and risotto (rice cooked in broth) with rapini (an Italian, mustardlike broccoli). The hallmarks of Italian cooking—appealing flavors, fresh ingredients, and robust seasonings—have made it America's favorite cuisine.

The lasagna "bar" appeals to many cooks. It allows guests to layer their own ingredients such as cooked pasta, soft cheeses, browned meat, roasted vegetables (such as carrots, sweet peppers, onions, and garlic), broccoli, tomato sauce, and Parmesan cheese.

The classic Italian bruschetta is a slice of toasted coarse bread, rubbed with a clove of fresh garlic and brushed with a fine olive oil, then sprinkled with salt. The coarser the bread the better. In Italy, these breads are then garnished with a number of toppings that vary from region to region. In Tuscany, for example, bruschetta is topped with white beans cooked with herbs and garlic.

They are also prepared with roasted pepper strips and sour cream and then topped with pepper, garlic, basil, and olive oil. Other combinations include chopped tomatoes, eggplant, and ricotta cheese. You can use olives, chopped onions, anchovies, Italian salami, or fava beans. Keep in mind that the basic ingredients for flavoring the bread are virgin olive oil, basil, and garlic.

You can use common American vegetable varieties in all Italian recipes, but increasingly, discerning cooks want to prepare dishes with authentic ethnic varieties. The ethnic varieties included here and in the other chapters on ethnic gardens can usually only be obtained through seed catalogs, not from supermarkets.

Italian Vegetable Varieties

Artichokes

Italians like artichokes almost as much as Americans do. We know a few cooks who are artists at creating pasta with artichokes and basil; fettuccine with artichoke sauce; and braised chicken, angel hair pasta, and artichokes.

The huge, grayish, deeply cut leaves of the artichoke plant add a touch of class to any garden. This plant is much too big for most kitchen gardens; it can spread to 4 feet across. Instead, try growing one plant in a flower bed or wine barrel where it can show off its foliage.

Artichoke Purple: An Italian variety with mild, sweet-tasting flower buds. Seed source: ORN PIN

Beans

The fat, flat Romano bean is a staple of the Italian cuisine, either as a side dish, lightly cooked, or as a basic ingredient in such dishes as bucatini with green beans, olives, tomatoes, and port. Another favorite is beans with porcini (pork) in a sherry vinaigrette. Swordfish cooked Tuscan style is often served with green beans. Here are a few Italian varieties to try.

Beans (Pole)

Romano (pole): No bean says Italian like this flat Romano with a robust flavor. They're wonderful sauteed in olive oil with a few sprigs of summer savory. These beans are about $5^1/_2$ inches long, and have flattened pods, with brown seeds. Romanos produce an abundant crop of beans. Seed source: ALL BURP BUT COM DEG FAR GAR HEN LED NIC ORG PIN PON RED SEE SEED THO TIL VER WILL

Spanish Giant Romano: A favorite variety of northern Italy. It is a longer, Romano type bean with vigorous vines that grow to 8 feet. Seed source: ORN

Yellow Annelino: An Italian heirloom variety with a distinctive flavor. This is a 3- to 4-inch long bean with a crescent curl shape. Seed source: COO ORG

Beans (Bush)

Bush Romano: This bush variety is the same delicious Italian flat bean as the Pole Romano, except the bush only grows 18 inches tall and the seeds are white. Seed source: STO

Green Ruler: A long, very flat, podded, Romano type bean with a spreading bushy vine. It has a slightly nutty flavor. The pods are bright green. Seed source: DEG

Romanette: The plant grows upright to 18 inches high. It has 5- to 6-inch-long, broad, flat pods with white seeds. Seed source: DEG

Roman Bush: 5- to 6-inch-long, flat pods with white oval seeds. Seed source: GUR ORG PIN STO

Sequoia: A deep purple podded bean with a Romano flavor. This variety will grow almost everywhere. Seed source: COO

Beets

Americans don't usually think of beets as Italian, but there are some varieties with Italian roots. Serve them as side dishes.

Chioggia: This is an Italian heirloom variety that has alternating rings of cherry red and creamy white. Delicious when picked fresh. Seed source: COO JOH NIC ORN PIN SEE SEED SHE SOU

Broccoli

Broccoli and Italian cuisine often go together.

Calabrese: This broccoli grows $2^1/_2$ to 3 feet tall, with a 5- to 6-inch bluish green head. Calabrese sprouts lots of side branches. Seed source: ABU BOU FAR JLH NIC PIN RED SEE SOU

Green Sprouting De Cicco: An 1890 Italian heirloom variety with a 3- to 6-inch, flat green head. Seed source: ALL COM DEG HIG JOH ORG ORN SOU TIL WIL

Raab: A pungent heirloom variety with no central head. Cut the budlets before the flowers appear. Seed source: BURP COM JLH LED NIC PIN SEE SHE

Rapine: It looks like mustard with many green side sprouts. Dime-sized buds with no heads. Seed source: DEG JOH LED STO TWI

Cabbage

Cabbage leaves can be used as a wrap for vegetable cannelloni (boiled pasta wrapped around a filling).

Cuore Di Bue: An unusual Italian variety with a tight, pointed, compact, dark green head. Seed source: JLH

Testa Di Ferro: This is an Italian savoy cabbage that has deep green crinkled leaves that form a loose head. Seed source: JLH

Cantaloupe

Italian cuisine often features melons of all sorts. Serve slices of melon wrapped with a thin strip of prosciuto as part of an antipasto. Try melon soup, and an array of desserts.

Gallicum: A round, greenish yellow Mediterranean melon with green flesh. It weighs about 2 to $2^1/_2$ pounds. Seed source: NIC VER

Mr. Ugly Muskmelon: An Italian melon with deep ribs, big warts, and rough rind. It may be ugly, but the salmon-colored flesh is very sweet. Seed source: GLE

Cardoon

Cardoon can grow 8 feet high and 3 to 4 feet wide. This is a relative of the artichoke, with long, serrated, gray green leaves. Instead of eating the flowers, you eat the fleshy leaves. To blanch, wrap the leaves in a newspaper or plastic and tie with twine.

Large Smooth: An Italian variety that has a smooth stalk. Italian cooks use it in many dishes. Seed source: DEG

Cauliflower

Cauliflower is used in many ways. Try Parmesan cheese and bacon with cauliflower.

Italian Purple Bronze: An Italian variety that turns dark green when cooked. Seed source: COM

Precoce Di Toscana: Large, creamy white Italian variety. Especially good when pickled. Seed source: JLH

Chard

Chard is good cooked or added to salad greens.

Argentata: Italian heirloom that has silvery white midribs and deep green, savoyed leaves. It has an extremely mild flavor. Seed source: SHE

Monstruoso: An Italian strain with broad, white stalks and smooth, dark green leaves. Seed source: COO

Radicchio (Chicory)

Radicchio can be used with salad

greens to add a touch of bitterness, or the leaves can be stuffed with goat cheese and served before a meal.

Adria: Italian chicory with crimson heads that weigh 9 ounces. Leaves have white veins. Seed source: STO TWI

Castelfranco: Italian heirloom variety that has marbled red-and-white coloring. Heads do not need cutting back to produce well. Seed source: COO

Milan: Traditional Italian radicchio has an 8-ounce, round, burgundy red head. Seed source: LED

Nerone De Treviso: An Italian nonforcing variety. Red-edged leaves have creamy white bases. Seed source: SHE

Radichetta: Italian variety that has toothed, curled, green leaves. $1^1/_2$- to 3-inch-wide stalks. Seed source: COM COO LED NIC SEE STO VER

Rossa Di Verona: Dark red Italian heirloom variety that has a slightly bitter taste. Seed source: ABU BOU VER

Cucumbers

Italian salads such as panszanella (bread salad) often call for cucumbers. Here are some varieties to try.

Bianco Lungo Di Parigi: A creamy white, very knobby variety. Seed source: PIN

Precoce Grosso Bianco Creama: Creamy white Italian variety grows to 5 by 2 inches. There is no bitter taste. Seed Source: RED

Eggplant

You often find eggplant in Italian dishes such as eggplant-zucchini parmigiana (prepared with Parmesan cheese) or grilled eggplant lasagna. You can also put together an eggplant cannelloni by replacing the traditional pasta wrappers with roasted eggplant slices to enclose a pork or carrot filling.

Vioetta Di Firenze: This Italian heirloom variety has large, oblong, pale violet fruit with fluted grooves. It needs plenty of heat to grow. Seed source: COO ORN PIN

Italian White: Grows round and plump. This variety will add a mushroomlike taste to Italian dishes. Seed source: Seed

Romanesca: Romanesca produces a large, oval, pinkish white fruit. Seed source: JLH

Garlic

Try any Italian dish such as pastina risotto (rice cooked with broth and grated cheese) and risotto primavera and you'll find that garlic is a staple of most Italian cooking. Garlic is easy to grow and care for.

Crushed or sliced garlic often has a strong, hot flavor when it's sprinkled on a salad. This is caused by two enzymes that mix to create a pungent taste. You can modify the taste of garlic by heating. Here's how:

Hot-pungent: Use fresh garlic, chopped or crushed, in salads.

Hardy flavor: Heat chopped garlic. This takes some of the sting out of the flavor. Cooked garlic is an essential ingredient in Italian sauces.

Mild: Simmer over a low heat until the cloves are soft. You can eat them whole or add them to other dishes.

Mild and Creamy: Roast full heads until tender. Mash and use them as a spread on bread.

Lorz Italian: A pre-1900 Italian heirloom variety. It averages 16 squarish-shaped cloves. Seed source: SOU

Chet's Italian Purple: A mild-flavored garlic with large bulbs that average 3 ounces each, with 15 cloves per bulb. It is a favorite of Italian cooks. Seed source: SOU

Kale

Kale is a wonderful winter vegetable. Use it in salads and Italian-style soups.

Lacinato Italian: An ornamental Italian heirloom variety that has 3-by-10-inch, straplike, blue green leaves. Most cooks use this variety as a garnish. Seed source: SHE

Onions

Italians use onions in almost everything from chicken-tortellini soup to tomato focaccia and spaghetti with clams. Here are some varieties to try.

Borettana: A pickling onion. This Italian heirloom has rosy bronze skin. Seed source: SHE

Italian Red: A spindle-shaped onion with purplish red scales and red flesh. It has a short storage life. These you can find in most supermarkets. Seed source: GUR HEN SEED

Italian Blood Red Bottle: A large, spindle-shaped onion with a spicy, tangy flavor. It is a favorite in Italy. Seed source: NIC

Peppers (Hot)

Many Italian cooks use hot peppers to add a flavorful twist to some of their traditional dishes. Try adding simmered tomatoes and peppers to a pasta for a tasty side dish.

Pepperoncini: A southern Italian variety that grows to 5 inches long. It is fiery red and mildly hot when fully ripe. Seed source: ABU HOR NIC ORN SHE

Peppers (Sweet)

Italians often roast red and yellow peppers and season them with basil and garlic. They can be garnished with shards of pecorino (an Italian cheese made from sheep's milk). Italian cooks also use sweet peppers extensively in recipes such as fontina cheese-and-rice stuffed peppers, or pasta with red pepper sauce.

Corno Di Toro Red: Italian heirloom variety that is mildly sweet and grows 6 to 12 inches long. Red when fully ripe. Seed source: COO GLE PIN SEED SHE TOMA

Cuneo: Pointed Italian variety grows to the size of a softball, but is pointed. It turns bright yellow when ripe. Seed source: PIN

Spinach

Spinach finds its way into many Italian dishes, such as baked spinach and ham frittata.

Italian Summer: Has green, savoyed leaves. It is a bolt-resistant, short-season variety. Seed source: SHE

Squash (Summer)

In midsummer when squash season is in full swing, Italy's Campo dei Fiorio market features zucchini and other summer squash of every description ranging from golden yellow to striped to round—and everything else in between. Italians often pick finger-sized zucchinis and saute them, dip the blossoms in batter and fry them, or sizzle summer squash slices on the grill. Zucchini flowers are delicious when stuffed with meat and fried. Pick the fullest flowers in the morning before they close. Wash and place them on paper towels to dry. Store them in a plastic bag. For peak flavor, use them the same day that they are picked.

Here are a few varieties to try.

Arlesa: Produces glossy green fruit that are perfect for sautéing when they are 4 to 8 inches long. Seed source: ORN SHE

Cocozelle Bush: Also called Italian Vegetable Marrow. Grows to 14 inches long, 5 inches thick, with greenish white flesh. For best flavor, pick young. Seed source: ALL DEG GAR HIG JOH LED NIC ORG PLA SEE SEED STO WILL

Costa Romesca: This Italian variety has a fruit that is 8 inches thick by 2 feet long. It is a fluted fruit that is usually fried whole with the flower still attached. Seed source: RED

Cuccuzze: An edible Italian gourd that grows 4 to 6 feet long (sometimes even longer) and weighs 8 to 15 pounds. It has a delicate "green" lemony taste, huge furry leaves, curling tendrils, and scented white flowers. In short summer areas, start the seeds indoors 1 to 12 weeks before planting outdoors. Gardeners in warm areas should plant the seed in the ground about 4 weeks before the last frost. Space seeds 8 to 10 inches apart. Harvest when they are between 15 and 25 inches long. Best grown up a fence where there is plenty of room. Seed source: COM DEG JLH

Fiorentino: Partial bush variety from Italy. Fruit is ridged, striped light and dark green, and grows 7 to 9 inches long. Seed source: SHE

Milano: Has shiny, dark green, speckled fruit. A good choice for sautéing. Seed source: BURR PAR WIL

Tondo di Nizza: A speckled, light green variety with superb texture and nutty flavor. The larger fruit are good stuffed. Seed source: BOU GOU SEED SHE

Zuchetta Rampicante: An Italian heirloom that grows 12 to 15 inches long and is often a curved trumpet shape. The blossoms are edible. Seed source: ORN PIN SHE

Tomatoes

Tortellini with rosemary tomato sauce, fettuccini with asparagus and tomatoes, grilled tomatoes with pesto, and pasta with spicy shrimp and tomato sauce are just a few Italian recipes to choose from when using tomatoes.

Costoluto Genovese: A slightly ribbed, scarlet tomato that grows 3 inches long and weighs about 5 ounces. A northern Italian heirloom variety. Seed source: RED SEE SEED SHE SOU TOMA

Milano: This determinate, red, plum-shaped tomato is used in many Italian dishes. Seed source: SHE TOM

San Remo: Red paste tomato grows on an indeterminate vine. Fat, elongated, sausage-shaped fruit. Seed source: SHE

Italian Herb Varieties

Italian dishes such as herbed warm pasta salad are known for their robust herb flavors and their use of basil, chives, oregano, sage, thyme, tarragon, and Italian parsley. Seafood lasagna, for instance, is enhanced by the use of rosemary. Oregano highlights spinach and ham manicotti. Pesto is a classic Italian sauce using basil, but you can add a combination of herbs for a tasty variety, such as basil-mint-orange pesto, creamy cilantro pesto, or lemon-thyme pesto.

Basil

Growing basil can easily become an obsession, making it the herb most closely associated with Italian cooking. Basil leaves are fragile and extremely aromatic. Karen grows enough basil each year to keep the fresh leaves coming all summer. In the fall, she pulls them off and dries the rest for winter use. Of course, once you've grown one Italian variety, you'll want to sample them all. Here are some favorites.

Italian Red Basil: Grows 15 inches tall and has deep red purple, highly aromatic leaves. Seed source: NIC

Licorice Basil: Has an aniselike aroma. Seed source: ABU COO PAR PIN RIC TAY VER

Napoletano Basil: A southern Italian variety with large, 2-by-3-inch, light green, deeply crinkled leaves. Use as a garnish in many Italian dishes. Seed source: RED SHE

Sweet Italian Large Leaf: Has extremely large leaves and is the one basil used to make pesto. Seed source: COM DEG GAR HIG PAR PIN RED TAY TIL

Fennel

The leaves and seeds of licorice-flavored fennel spice up salads, eggs, fish, and sauces. The bulbous base can also be steamed, grilled, or served raw. Italian cooks say that the flavor blends well with chicken and squash. You'll find it used in many dishes, such as fennel parmigiana.

Florence Fennel: Also called Finocchio or Sweet Florence. Grows 36 to 60 inches tall and has enlarged, flat, oval, celerylike leaves. It has a licorice-anise flavor. Seed source: BOU BURP COM DEG HEN JUN LED LIB NIC PIN POR SEE SOU STO TWI VER WILL

Wild Fennel: Has large, fleshy leaves with a distinctive flavor. Seed source: ABU

Mint

Mint can be found growing profusely in the Mediterranean region. Mint in the Italian kitchen is almost always used in fresh form and adds a unique flavor to fish, poultry, fruit, and vegetables. The mints most used by American cooks are peppermint, spearmint, and applemint. In Italy, mint is popular as a garnish for desserts and as a flavoring in sherbet.

Roman Mint: Found growing wild near Rome. Has the flavor of menthol, spearmint, and pennyroyal. Seed source: RIC

Oregano

Oregano is often used dried rather than fresh in such dishes as zucchini rice tart, spinach and ham manicotti, and marinated mozzarella. It is intensively aromatic and can take over your garden if it's not confined.

Italian Oregano: An Italian variety with a strong flavor. Seed source: DAB NIC RIC SEED

Parsley

You'll find Italian parsley in such dishes as Tuscan white panzanella, stuffed turbot (flounder fish), shrimp, and cauliflower insalata (an Italian marinated salad). Parsley is used frequently as a garnish in many Italian dishes. Because of its strong flavor, many chefs use Italian parsley in soups, pasta, and meat dishes.

Italian: Has celerylike, glossy, dark-green leaves. Its flavor is much stronger than traditional parsley. Seed source: DAB GOU HIG MEY PIN SEED TAY TER WILL

Italian Giant: Grows to 3 feet tall and has a plain green leaf. This variety has an extremely strong flavor. Seed source: COO ORN NIC RED SEE

Rosemary

Rosemary is a Mediterranean native that has literally taken over America. Cooks use it to flavor barbecued meats, vinegars, and sauces. Our different varieties of rosemary have given us years of aromatic delights in the kitchen.

Corisican Prostrate: A prostrate rosemary with dark blue flowers. Seed source: RIC

Tuscan Blue: Grows 6 feet high, erect, with large blue flowers. Seed source: RIC

Thyme

Thyme is a staple ingredient throughout the Mediterranean. It is traditional in Italian sauces.

Oregano Thyme: Has the scent of oregano. It is a creeping variety with an excellent flavor. Seed source: RIC

Chapter Eight

The Oriental Kitchen Garden

Oriental cooking has always fascinated American cooks since it emphasizes fresh vegetables, or a combination of vegetables and meat. For centuries China has been famous for its variety of cuisine. In Canton, for instance, popular dishes are sweet potato and carrot soup, steamed chicken and mustard greens, pork-filled chilies, and bitter melons with a black bean mix. In Beijing, you'll find gingered tomatoes, and pork with garlic chives.

The only difficult part of Oriental cooking is in understanding which vegetables go with names like *dai gai choy, bok choy, siew choy,* and *gai lohn.* All of these vegetables are relatives of mustard, broccoli, and cabbage. Freshness is absolutely essential in preparing oriental dishes, especially with stir-fry.

Creating Stir-Fries

Using a Wok

Woks were created in China more than a thousand years ago. If you prepare the food at the table, wok cooking becomes high drama. Pick 2 or 3 cups of vegetables fresh directly from the garden, and slice or shred them. Heat the wok until hot, and then pour in one tablespoon of peanut (or other) oil and crushed garlic. Add the vegetables, and stir-fry 3 to 4 minutes. Season with herbs and 1 to 2 tablespoons of soy sauce. Stir-fry 1 minute more to blend the flavors. Here are some general tips about woks:

- A wok is a perfect shape for even-heat cooking and constant stir-ring. It also behaves nicely on the table.
- Stir-frying is great fun, but you can also steam or deep-fry directly in the wok.
- Flat-bottom woks are suitable for electric ranges; a wok with a ring works on gas ranges.
- Never substitute butter or shortening for peanut or vegetable oil.
- Pat vegetables dry on a paper towel before popping them into your wok. Wet vegetables splatter in hot grease and don't stir-fry well.

Oriental Vegetables

Some of these oriental vegetables are available in supermarkets, but if you really want to know what oriental vegetables taste like, you need to grow your own. We always have an oriental garden during fall and winter (Figure 8-1).

Burdock (Gobo)

This Japanese specialty is used in many oriental dishes. The plant has long stalks, broad leaves, and sharp burrs. Plant burdock seeds $\frac{1}{4}$ inch deep and 2 to 3 inches apart. Keep the soil moist during the germination period. The root is edible; scrape, scald, and boil it.

Seed source: ABU JOH SUN

Takingoama: Long slender 32-inch roots. Seed source: ABU JOH SON

Michihili Oriental Long Cabbage (Fall / Spring)	Edible Podded Peas (Spring)		
Pepper California Wonder (Sweet) (Summer)	Broccoli Shogun (Spring)	Peas (Spring) Eggplant Ichiban (Summer)	Eggplant Asian Bride (Summer)
Garlic (Spring)	Pak-Choi (Spoon Shaped) Mustard Cabbage (Fall / Spring)	Pak-Choi (Spoon Shaped) Mustard Cabbage (Fall / Spring)	Gai Choy (Mustard Flavored Leaves) (Fall / Spring)
Onions (Spring) Carrots (Fall / Spring)			Michihili Oriental Long Cabbage (Fall / Spring)

Figure 8-1. Oriental garden. 4' x 4' bed.

Chinese Broccoli/Chinese Kale (Gai Lohn)

The dark green leaves and stems look and taste like broccoli, but the stalks are tougher and need to be peeled before cooking. It matures in 70 days. Plant seeds $1/2$ inch deep and 3 inches apart. Thin the seedlings to stand 6 inches apart when 2 inches tall.

Seed source: SUN

Chinese Cabbage (Siew Choy)

The plant produces a compact head that looks like a cross between regular cabbage and romaine lettuce. There are two types: michihili, the tall one, and napa (wong bok), the barrel-shaped cabbage. Sow seeds directly in the beds about 4 inches apart, or start them in pots. Thin or transplant seedlings to stand 12 to 13 inches apart. When the plants are 5 to 8 inches tall, tie their leaves loosely to help form heads. Harvest when the heads are firm. Here are some varieties to try.

Michihili Type

Michihili type cabbage is tall and slender.

Jade Pagoda: Heads are about 16 inches by 5 inches thick. Deep green, broad, and compact head. Seed source: LED MEY PAR POR STU

Michihili: 4 to 6-pound head, 18 by 4 inches. Dark green. Seed source: ABU ALL BURR BUT COM DEG FAR GAR GUR JUN LED MEY NIC PIN POR ROS SOU STO SUN TWI WIL WILL

South China Earliest: 1-pound head, 10 by 14 inches tall. Japanese variety that is creamy white and tender. Seed source: GLE JOH RED

Napa Type

Napa type cabbage is squat, barrel shaped, and heavy.

China Pride: $5^1/_2$-pound head. Seed source: ORN STO TWI

Orient Express: A small, solid, oblong head. Seed source: BURP

Wong Bok: 5- to 7-pound head, 7 to 10 inches tall, light green. Drought resistant. Seed source: COM DEG NIC SUN

Chinese Celery (Heun Kunn)

This slow-growing plant forms an 8-inch-wide clump or leafy celerylike stalks. It is fragrant and delicious. Sow seeds in early spring in pots. Transplant 4 weeks later into the kitchen garden. Space the plants 8 inches apart.

Chinese Kan-Tsai: Oriental celery that has long, slender, dark green stems with a strong flavor. Seed source: ABU DEG HIG VER

Crispy Spears: 18-inch-long, crispy stalks. Easy to grow. Seed source: PAR

Chinese Chives (Gow Choy)

This member of the onion family gives off a hint of garlic. Sow seeds directly in the ground 10 inches apart. Cut the tops when they are 5 to 6 inches high. Continue cutting throughout the season. There is one variety.

Seed source: ABU BURP COM COO DAB DEG GAR GOU HEN HIB JOH JUN LED LEJ NIC ORG ORN PAR PIN RED RIC SEE SEED SHE SOU SUN TER THE THO TIL VER WILL

Chinese Mustard Cabbage (Bok Choy, Bok Choi)

Bok choy is the general name for loose-leaf, nonheading Chinese cabbage. This is a slim "cabbage" that grows upright with spoon-shaped leaves. 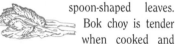 Bok choy is tender when cooked and has a stronger flavor than the regular Chinese cabbage.

Plant bok choy in early spring in cooler areas and in the fall in warmer climates. Sow $\frac{1}{2}$ inch apart and thin the larger type to 10 inches apart. Because it grows upright, it can be grown as close as 2 inches apart if you harvest and eat the seedlings as you thin the plants. You can grow fairly large quantities in a container. It develops tender heads in about 40 days. Young leaves are great in salads and for stir-frying. The young heads are good steamed and buttered.

Too much temperature variation or temperatures that are too hot or too cold cause bok choy to go to seed. We like to plant it in early fall and let it mature as the temperatures drop. Add compost and manure to the bed before seeding.

Bok Choi: Thick, green leaves and broad, white stalks. Seed source: GUR HEN LIB NIC SEED STO SUN THE

Joi-Choi: 12 to 15 inches tall, dark green leaves with white stalks. Seed source: JOH JUN NIC PAR STO TER VER

Pak Choi: Smooth, rounded, green leaves with white stems. Seed source: ABU HIG JOH SUN TIL

Oriental Parsley (Yuen Sai)

The leaves and stems of this plant are also called *cilantro*. They have a strong distinctive flavor and fragrance. The seeds are known as *coriander* and are used as an herb. Sow seeds in place in early spring, then thin the plants to stand 7 to 10 inches apart.

Chinese Parsley: Grows to 14 inches tall. The leaves are used extensively in Chinese cooking. Seed source: NIC SUN

Vietnamese Coriander: A Vietnamese variety that grows well in a pot. Seed source: RIC

Chinese Spinach (Hinn Choy)

Some varieties of Chinese spinach have green, red, and red-streaked leaves. It has a mild flavor. Start seeds indoors, and set out 4 inches apart in mid-spring.

Entsai: Also called water spinach. Mild, long leaves on 12-inch stems. Seed source: PIN

Hinn Choy: Small, fuzzy, green paddle-shaped leaves have tangy flavor. Seed source: ABU JOH NIC THE

Imperial Express: Smooth, medium green leaves. Seed source: VER

Orient Spinach: Smooth, dark green leaves. Seed source: SUN

Chop Suey Green (Shunguki)

This is also called Garland Chrysanthemum, and we've had good luck growing it in our winter beds. This plant grows to 3 feet tall if it's allowed to flower. It has lobed aromatic leaves that are used in stir-fries and soup. Sow seeds $1/4$ inch deep and 6 inches apart. Thin to 10 inches apart. Harvest before flowering.

Seed source: ABU BOU COO GAR GLE HIG JOH NIC PIN SEE STO SUN TER THE VER

Onions (Ha Ske Ko)

Plant $^1/_2$ inch deep and 2 to 3 inches apart.

Oriental Bunching: A Japanese variety. This onion has been bred for crispness and mild flavor. It has a green, tubular stalk and a long, slender white head. Use the whole plant in stir-fries. Seed source: ALL BOU COM FAR GUR HEN JLH JUN NIC PIN SEE STO THE VER

Oriental Beans

Oriental beans are a group of beans that many cooks already grow. Yard Long beans are not actually a bean, even though they look like a bean and grow like a bean. Plant seeds $^1/_4$ inch deep and 6 inches apart. Harvest when the beans are tender, about 6 inches long. Place Mung bean seeds in a quart jar, and soak them overnight. Turn the jar on its side for three days. Rinse the beans regularly. If grown to maturity, Mung beans will produce 3-inch curving pods with white seeds. Plant 4 to 6 inches apart.

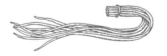

Adzuke: A shell bean with a 5-inch-long pod. Dark red rounded seeds have a nutty flavor. Used extensively in Chinese cooking. Seed source: JLH JOH PIN RED SUN VER

Mung Beans (Low Dow): They are very popular sprout beans and are used in salads. Seed source: ABU DEG HEN LED PAR PIN POR SEE VER WIL

Yard Long Asparagus Bean (Dok Gopuk): It is vining and has 1- to 2-foot-long pods with thick, crisp skins. Seed source: SEE SOU SUN

Oriental Cucumbers

These are longer, thinner, and crisper than conventional cucumbers. Grow these on supports and plant 6 to 12 inches apart.

China Long Green: A 20- to 24-inch-long light green cucumber. Seed source: COM FAR

Chinese Snake: Dark green, long, and curved. Seed source: SEE

Oriental Eggplant

These are long, narrow fruit. They are usually steamed or cooked in mixed vegetable dishes. Start them indoors, and then plant outdoors when the soil warms. Plant 12 to 18 inches apart.

Chinese Long: a $1^3/_4$-inch-thick, 10-inch-long, purple variety. Seed source: GLE THE

Little Fingers: Long, glossy dark purple fruit grows in clusters. Seed source: SHE

Osaka Honnoa: $7^1/_2$ inches, purple fruit. Seed source: SOU

Oriental Melons

Oriental melons are more like squash than melons. There are four types to try: bitter melon, fuzzy melon, winter melon, and sponge gourd. Oriental melons are warm-weather vegetables that need plenty of water, rich soil, and warm, sunny weather. Grow them up a fence to keep the vines compact.

Balsam Pear (Foo Gwa): A 2-by-8-inch melon with light green flesh. Looks much like a warty cucumber. Soak the fruit in salt water to help leach out the bitterness before cooking. Seed source: SUN

Bitter Melon (Moh Gwah): Grows about 1 foot in diameter and matures

in 90 days. Most cooks pick them when they are immature. The melon at this stage can be peeled, sliced, and cooked in butter, or stuffed and baked as you would zucchini. Seed source: SUN

Chinese Winter Melon (Doon Gwah): Is the base of winter melon soup. You can hollow the melon out and steam the soup inside. It grows to about the size of a pumpkin and looks like a watermelon with firm white flesh. Store to use throughout the winter. You will need to support the melons with a cloth sling and grow them up a fence or trellis. Harvest after melons reach pumpkin size. Seed source: SUN

Early Silver Line: Elongated, white-fleshed melon. Yellow silvery furrowed rind is so thin it can be peeled. Seed source: BURP

Sprite: 1-pound, all-white melon. Skin turns yellowish when mature. Seed source: PIN

Sponge Gourd

Sponge gourd (See Gwah): The gourds grow 6 to 12 inches long and have a delicate sweet taste. The flavor is a cross between a cucumber and a summer squash. Remove the ridges before using. Stir-fry with chunks of chicken or shrimp. Cut into chunks to simmer for soup. As the gourds overmature, their ridges turn brown and their flesh becomes spongy and inedible. Seed source: SUN

Oriental Mustard (Gai Choy)

Oriental mustard has a strong taste with a touch of bitterness. Some varieties produce heads or semiheads in cold weather. Sow seeds $1/_4$-inch deep and 4 inches apart. Thin to stand 8 inches apart.

Autumn Poem: Bright green, broccolilike plant produces edible flowers, stalks, young buds, and leaves. If cut back, it will produce all summer. Seed source: PIN

Canton Dwarf Pak Choy: Looks like an immense head of lettuce. Seed source: DEG

Chinese Stem Mustard: Light green, serrated leaves are 8 inches long and 2 inches wide. Seed source: STO

Chinese Tsi Shim: Light green leaves and flowering stalks. Harvest when flowers begin to open. Seed source: GAR SUN

Oriental Peas (Edible Podded)

The pods are completely edible and show up in many oriental dishes. Good cooks consider them a delicacy.

Snow Pea (Ho Lohn): Rich green pods are on a $2^1/_2$-foot plant. Seed source: BOU

Oriental Radishes

The varieties of Oriental radishes are classified as spring, summer/fall, or winter. They vary in root shape, size, skin, and flesh color.

April Cross (Daikon): Grows 14 to 18 inches long, 2 inches thick. It is pungent and white. Spring variety. Seed source: BURP BUT COM GAR GUR HEN NIC SUN THE TIL TWI VER

Black Spanish Round: A winter variety, globe-shaped with $3^1/_2$-inch diameter. Black skin with white pungent flesh. 1824 heirloom variety.

Seed source: BOU COM DEG FAR GUR JLH JUN LED LIB MEY SEE SOU STO VER WILL

Chinese Rose: 7 by 2 inches long. Has rose to light pink skin. Pungent white flesh. Seed source: DEG HEN JLH JUN LED MEY NIC PIN POR SEE SOU STO SUN VER

Green Long: Sow in fall. 15 by 2 inches long, green skin and flesh. Seed Source: SUN

Little Tokyo Round: 2 by 3 inches long and turnip shaped. Mild and crisp. Spring variety. Seed source: TER

Chapter Nine

The Mexican Kitchen Garden

Everyone is familiar with tacos, burritos, or tortillas, but Mexican cooking extends far beyond that. The heart of Mexican cooking is the infinite variety of its salsas and sauces that provide much of the flavor. The most characteristic seasoning in Mexican cuisine is the chili (hot pepper), which adds flavors to dishes ranging from Mole Colorado de Oaxaca to Chilaquiles con Salsa verde.

Mexican Cooking
Chilies

Today there are more than 140 varieties of chilies grown in Mexico and the United States. Chilies carry varying degrees of pungent spiciness and range in color from pale green to yellow, orange, red, purple, brown, or black. Sizes range from large to small, but generally speaking, the smaller the pepper, the hotter the taste.

In 1902, pharmacologist Wilbur Scoville mixed ground chilies, sugar, alcohol, and water and taste-tested their heat content. He gave each chili a value depending on how much water was needed to eliminate the heat. Today's computerized technology rates peppers from 0, the mildest, to 200,000, the hottest. Some scales rate these peppers from 0 to 10. A green bell pepper would be rated 0; a Habanero pepper would be rated 10 (or about 200,000 units on the Scoville scale).

The heat in a chili is consolidated in the interior veins. Yellowish orange veins indicate that the chili is extra hot. The seeds also contain a great deal of heat. Chilies vary in their heat content from variety to variety and with the growing conditions. Hot dry areas produce hotter chilies. See Table 9-1 for a general rundown.

To roast chilies, place the chiles on the grill (Anaheims are a favorite). Turn them frequently until the skins are evenly blackened and charred all over. Put chilies in a paper bag for a few minutes to cool and steam. Peel the charred skins and then cut and remove veins and seeds. Use chiles to make salsa and other Mexican dishes.

Mexican cuisine also features corn, beans, tomatoes, tomatillos, onions, squash, jicamas, and chayotes. You can grow adequate quantities of all of these in a 4-by-4-foot kitchen garden, in a portion of a flower bed, or in a combination of postage stamp beds and containers. See Figure 9-1 for a sample Mexican garden.

Salsas (Sauces)

Salsa is the Mexican word for *sauces* (usually hot). They can be added to almost any food and are always a creation waiting to happen. Kitchen gardening cooks now spice up these salsas to tongue-tingling perfection by combining sweet fruit, avocados, and other ingredients. Try one of the following with jalapeño peppers: peaches, apricots, tomatillos, avocado, sweet peppers, tomatoes, green beans, black beans, or any other combination that strikes your fancy.

Also experiment with combinations of bell peppers, garlic, and onions with parsley, cilantro, and/or oregano. While jalapeño peppers are usually

CHILI	HEAT CONTENT	SCOVILLE UNITS
Anaheim	Varies from mild to slightly warm	1,000–2,000
Poblano (Ancho)	Mild to slightly warm	2,000–4,000
Yellow Wax (Caribe, Goldspike, Santa Fe Grande)	Warm to hot	6,000
Fresno	Hot to hotter	About 10,000
Jalapeño	Hot to look out!	About 10,000
Serrano	Wow!	35,000
Habanero	Explosive	150,000 plus

TABLE 9-1. CHILIES RATED ON THE SCOVILLE SCALE

the choice for salsas, there are hundreds of chili varieties, each of which contributes a different flavor and level of hotness.

Here is a general recipe:

4 pounds Roma tomatoes, coarsely chopped
1 pound tomatillos, husked and chopped
4 large sweet peppers (any color), coarsely chopped
3 large onions, coarsely chopped
6 jalapeño peppers (or other varieties), seeded and minced
1 bunch cilantro, chopped
4 cloves garlic (or more to taste)
2 tablespoons sugar (optional)

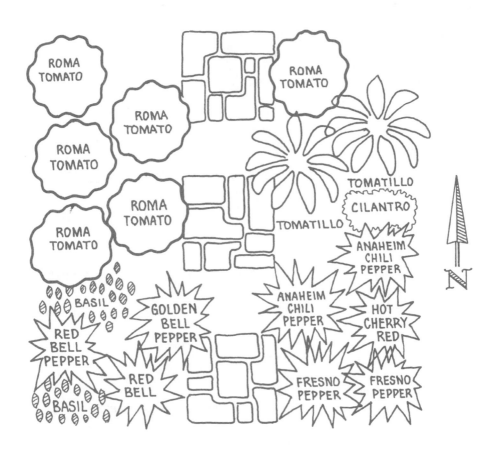

Figure 9-1. Mexican garden. 4' x 4' bed.

For green tomatillo salsa, try this recipe:

> *10 tomatillos, diced*
> *$\frac{1}{3}$ cup chopped fresh cilantro*
> *2 jalapeño peppers, seeded and minced*
> *$\frac{3}{4}$ cup regular-strength chicken broth*
> *2 teaspoons lime juice*
> *$\frac{1}{2}$ cup chopped onion*

To make either salsa, just mix all the ingredients together. (Keep the salsa refrigerated.)

The critical ingredient common to all successful salsas is freshness. Salsa prepared with ingredients harvested from your own garden always has a flavor and character lacking in commercial salsas.

Salsas are spooned over meats, tacos, eggs, and beans or served as a dip with corn chips. Salsas made with red ripe tomatoes are called *salsa rojas*. Salsa made from tomatillos, which are green, are called *salsa verdes*. For salsa roja, we suggest you grow tomatoes, several varieties of chilies, onion, garlic, cilantro, and oregano. Some cooks like to add other ingredients, such as cucumbers, radishes, or zucchini. For salsa verde, you will need tomatillos, jalapeño chilies, garlic, onion, and cilantro.

We suggest you experiment with your salsa garden. You might start by collecting salsa recipes and then planting a basic salsa garden that consists of one tomatillo plant, three or four tomato plants, two or three hot pepper plants, one or two sweet pepper, and as many herbs as you can squeeze in. A good salsa garden might consist of three wine barrels planted with tomatoes, chiles, and a tomatillo, or a piece of flower bed planted to accommodate your favorite salsa recipe. Don't be afraid to

164

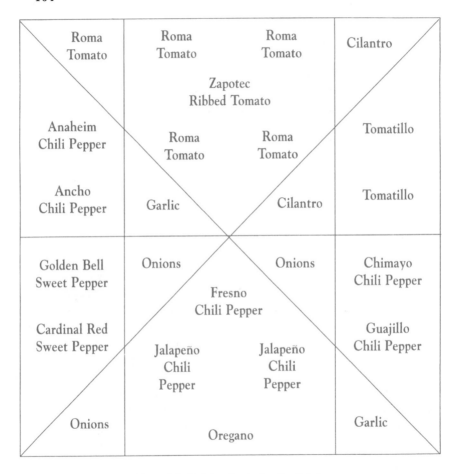

Figure 9-2. Mexican salsa garden. 4' x 4' bed.

experiment with different varieties and types of vegetables. Figure 9-2 is a sample of a salsa garden.

Mexico's Regal Sauce: Mole

Every good cook will want to try and serve a mole, a combination of roasted chiles, roasted vegetables, chocolate, and a variety of seasonings. This is a universal Mexican dish, yet each province has its own favorite mole. Cooks usually select ancho, guajillo, or pastilla as the chiles to roast, and onion, garlic, tomatoes, and tomatillos as the vegetables to roast. They combine herbs such as oregano, thyme, and marjoram with a variety of fruit and nuts.

Southwestern Cooking

While similar to Mexican cuisine, southwestern cooking has a distinct flavor all its own. The roots of southwestern cooking lie in Texas, New Mexico, and Arizona, where local chefs substituted ingredients in typical Mexican recipes that were indigenous to the southwest region. This type of cooking can go from bland to hot and spicy. The most basic ingredients in both Mexican and southwestern dishes are corn and chiles (hot peppers).

Mexican/Southwestern Vegetables

If you want a garden that will allow you to raise a general variety of vegetables that can be used in Mexican cooking, as well as in other cuisines, plant from the first varieties listed under each vegetable. If you are a cook who insists on authentic or southwestern varieties, plant from the specialized varieties.

Beans

You can use pinto beans or black beans in most Mexican dishes. The problem with these beans is that it takes a lot of vine to produce a good crop. Grow them on a bean tower, or in a long, narrow flower bed.

Midnight Black Turtle: This is a small black bean used for soup and as refried beans. Heavy yields on a bush that doesn't spread. Seed source: ABU GAR JOH ORG PIN RED SEE SHE

Pinto: Pinto beans have a long, broad, 5-inch oval pod. The seed is light buff speckled with greenish brown. Pintos are popular in all Mexican cooking. Seed source: ABU DEG HEN LED PAR PIN POR SEE VER WIL

Specialized Mexican/ Southwestern Bean Varieties

More and more cooks and specialized restaurants are serving heirloom beans native to the Southwest and Mexico. These beans, with such descriptive names as Anasazi and Montezuma Red Twiner, are varieties that date back hundreds of years. Long touted in health food circles for their nutritional value, dried beans, such as these southwestern/Mexican natives are gaining status in the gourmet world. These need space to produce quantities.

Anasazi: These mottled beans are red and white. Great bakers. Seed source: ABU PLA SEED VER

Aztec: Called a potato bean because the large white seeds are about the size of limas. Plant has short 3-foot runners. Seed source: PLA SEED

Aztec Red Kidney: Bush type that produces large, dark red kidney beans. An heirloom variety. Seed source: ABU

Frijol En Seco: A New Mexican variety. This bush pinto tolerates drought and poor soil conditions. Seed source: PLA

Montezuma Red Twiner: A smooth, red, faintly sweet waxy bean. Seed source: NIC

Sonoran Tepary Bean: Native to the Sonoran Desert and is 30 percent crude protein. 3-inch-long pods with small golden brown seeds. Seed source: PLA RED SEED

Corn

Extra Early Golden Bantam: This variety produces 5- to 6-inch ears on a 5-foot stalk. A good general variety with both Mexican and other cuisines. Seed source: **ALL GAR HIG WIL**

Golden Cross Bantam: 8-inch ears on a 7-foot stalk. Seed source: **BURP EAR GUR PON POR ROS VER WIL**

Specialized Mexican/ Southwestern Corn Varieties

Aztec: 6-inch ears, 12 rows of bright yellow kernels on a 5-foot stalk. Seed source: **STO**

Dry Field Corn (Grinding Corn)

Alamo-Navajo Blue Corn: Drought-tolerant variety. Produces large, full ears of dark bluish purple to almost black kernels. Seed source: **PLA**

Anasai: An ancient Native American variety. The 6- to 9-foot stalk produces multiears with multicolored kernels. Seed source: **SEED**

Apache Red: Apache Indian heirloom variety that grows to 6 feet tall. The ears produce black to reddish kernels. Seed source: **SEED**

Taos Blue: Grows to 8 feet tall. 20-inch ears produce 14 to 16 rows of blue kernels. Seed source: **RED**

Jicama

Jicama is a sweet, crisp root vegetable sold by street vendors in Mexico. When you buy Jicama slices, the vendor sprinkles them with lime juice and chili powder. The plant is 4 to 5 feet tall and the root weighs 1 to 5 pounds and is 4 to 8 inches in diameter. It has sandy-colored skin and white flesh. Requires a long hot growing season. One variety.

Seed source: DEG HEN NIC ORN RED SUN

Onions

Onions are used extensively in Mexican dishes such as Cabollas Yucatecas (onions Yucatan-style), Chayotes Rellenos (stuffed chayotes), and others.

Early Yellow Globe: A deep yellow onion with pure white flesh. This is a mild-flavored onion. Seed source: **ABU DEG FAR JUN PIN SOU STO TER VER WILL**

*Specialized Mexican/
Southwestern Onion Varieties*

New Mexico Yellow: Top-shaped with light yellow scales and soft white, mild flesh. Seed source: **ABU WIL**

Zapotec: 3- to 4-inch-diameter, Spanish type onion. Stores well. Seed source: **BURR**

Zuni: 4- to 5-inch-diameter, Spanish type onion that can be tucked into a corner of a kitchen garden. Seed source: **BURR**

Chilies (Peppers, Medium to Hot)

The most characteristic seasoning in Mexican cuisine is the chili. You'll find it in a multitude of dishes ranging from Chiles Rellenos de Queso (cheese-stuffed chiles) to Enchiladas de Jalba (crab enchiladas).

To make a chili wreath for the kitchen, buy a wreath base from a craft shop. Using a needle and coarse thread, pierce beneath the stem of any variety of dried red chilies. Select the heat content and variety that suits your taste. String the chilies, and form into a circle to fit the wreath base. You can mount several chili strings on the base. Secure them to the base with florist pins and raffia. When you want to use the chilies, break them off and remove stem. Add them to any recipe calling for chilies.

The following five chiles can be used in most Mexican cooking.

Anaheim: Long, green, mild chiles used extensively in Mexican and southwestern cooking. Adds mild heat to all kinds of Mexican dishes. Seed source: **ABU COO DEG HOR JLH PIN POR RED SEE SEED SHE SOU WIL**

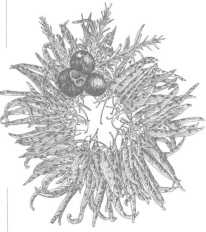

Chili wreath.

Ancho: Plump, heart-shaped, medium-hot, blackish green chili. Anchos have a rich flavor with a touch of bitterness. Seed source: BURP HEN HOR NIC PIN PLA RED SEE SEED SHE

Guero: Small, yellow chili, often called a wax chili. Seed source: BURR DEG HOR ORN PLA RED ROS WIL

Jalapeño: Thick-fleshed, small, cylindrical, very hot pepper about 1 inch across and 2 to 3 inches long. Used extensively in sauces. Seed source: BURR BUT COM COO DEG FIS GLE GUR HEN HOR NIC PLA PON POR RED ROS SEE SEED SOU STO SUN

Serrano: A small, cylindrical, 2-by-3-inch, dark green chili. Hot, hot, and hot. Wear gloves, wash your hands when cutting or peeling, and keep your fingers away from your mouth and eyes. Mexican cooks use them in very hot sauces. Seed source: BURP COO DEG GUR HEN

HOR PIN PLA POR RED ROS SEE SEED SHE TER WIL

Specialized Mexican/ Southwestern Chili Varieties

Chimayo: A New Mexican native. Long, thin, curved chili that turns from green to red when ripe. Seed source: PLA RED

Guajillo: Comes from Mexico. Hot. $4\frac{1}{2}$ to 6 inches long and $\frac{1}{4}$ inch in diameter. Seed source: PLA RED

Sonora: A mildly pungent, Anaheim type. Pods are 8 inches long and $\frac{1}{2}$ inch in diameter. They turn from green to red when fully ripe. Seed source: TOMA

Cylindrical Peppers

Ancho San Luis: A mildly pungent variety. Pods are 6 inches long by 3 inches in diameter. It turns from dark green to red. Seed source: JLH TOMA

Early Jalapeño: The pods are 3 inches long by $\frac{1}{2}$ inch in diameter. It turns from deep green to red when ripe. Early Jalapeño is extremely hot. Seed source: ABU BURR DEG GAR

HIG JOH JUN PIN PER SHE TER TIL WIL

Guajillo Casteno: This is one hot pepper. The pods are 3 inches long and tapered; they have thin walls. Turns translucent red when ripe. Seed source: SEED

Ole!: A giant jalapeño type pepper that is very hot. Seed source: NIC

Puya: This means *spur* in Spanish. This chili grows upward on a 2-foot plant, and the pods are tapered. $3^1/_2$ inches long by 1 inch in diameter. Seed source: JLH JOH SUN

Relleno: This is the one used by good cooks in the famous Chili Relleno recipe. The pods grow $6^1/_2$ inches long by $2^1/_2$ inches in diameter and turn from green to red when fully ripe. It is mildly hot. Seed source: HEN NIC SEED

Santo Domingo Pueblo: A New Mexican native that produces 2-inch-long by 1-inch-diameter conical pods. It is hot! Seed source: RED

Super Chili: A 15-inch plant that is ideal for the postage stamp kitchen garden. The pods are $2^1/_2$ inches long by $1/_2$ inch in diameter and are cone shaped. Hot chili. Seed source: COM

GUR HEN LIB ORN PAR SHE TOMA TWI VER WILL

Small Peppers

Cochiti: This chili is centuries old and was developed by the Cochiti Pueblo people along the Rio Grande in New Mexico. Pods are medium long and hot. Seed source: PLA

Red Chili: Extremely pungent. The pods are 3 inches long by $1/_2$ inch in diameter. They turn from green to red. Seed source: DEG FAR LED RED

Yellow Peppers

Santa Fe Grande: An extremely hot pepper. The pods turn from yellow to orange red when fully ripe. Seed source: BURR DEG HOR ORN PLA RED ROS WIL

Square/Round/Clawlike/Tiny Peppers

Habanero: A very hot Mexican variety that has to be handled carefully. Wear gloves, and keep the peppers away from your eyes and mouth. The pods turn from green to golden orange

when ripe. Seed source: BURP BURR COM DEG HOR LED LIB MEY NIC ORN PLA POR ROS STO TWI

Tepin: A southwestern variety that is literally the hottest pepper known. It is small and round. Seed source: RED SEE

Pumpkins

Pumpkins are used in Mexican desserts and soups. A bush variety is best for the postage stamp kitchen garden.

Bush Spirit: A 10- to 15-pound, 12-inch-diameter, yellow-fleshed pumpkin. Grows on 4-foot vines. Seed source: BURG COM DEG GUR HEN JUN LED LIB NIC ORN POR STO TER TWI

Specialized Mexican/Southwestern Pumpkin Varieties

Hopi Pale Grey: Has pale grey, nearly white rind and yellow flesh. The pumpkins weigh 5 to 10 pounds. Seed source: JLH

Squash

Squash seeds are ground for sauces, and squash flowers are battered and fried or placed into soups with the cubed squash.

Golden Dawn II: Bush-type, golden yellow. A zucchini-type squash. Seed source: GAR PAR

Specialized Mexican/Southwestern Squash Varieties

Acoma Squash: An ancient southwestern, winter variety that produces 10- to 15-pound squash that have thick, orange flesh. Seed source: PLA

Santo Domingo Squash: The fruit of this winter squash weighs 12 pounds and has pale yellow flesh and a green striped rind. Keep in a cool, dry place to store. Seed source: PLA

Tatume: A pear-shaped, summer squash that grows to 6 inches long and has a tough, green skin. Seed source: HOR POR

Texas Indian Moschata: Winter squash shaped like a flattened pumpkin. Weighs 10 to 15 pounds at maturity. It produces a large vine, so plant it by itself in a long flower bed. Seed source: **SEED**

Tomatillos

These are small, firm, round green fruit that are members of the tomato family. The fruit is covered with a paperlike husk, which is removed before cooking. Tomatillos are used extensively in salsas and sauces. Every Mexican postage stamp kitchen garden needs at least one tomatillo plant. Karen usually plants two. At the end of the season, she removes all of the tomatillos, pulls the husks off, boils them briefly, and purees them in the blender. She then freezes them until she wants to make a sauce during the winter months.

Mexican Strain: This variety produces 2-inch fruit. Seed source: TER

Tomatillo: A generic name for Toma Verde, Mexican Green, Green Husk, or Tomato Verde. Produces 2-inch fruit on tall, spindly plants that need to be caged. Seed source: ABU BURP COM COO GAR HEN JOH LIB PIN PLA POR RED SEE SEED SOU TER TIL TOMA VER WIL

Tomatoes

Tomatoes are the most important ingredient in Mexican cooking, right behind chilies. You can squeeze up to six plants into a 4-by-4-foot kitchen garden, along with a number of other vegetables.

Better Bush: Produces deep red, 4-inch fruit. Can be grown almost anywhere. Seed source: PAR

Husky Cherry Red: This dark red variety is a dwarf indeterminate plant that produces 1-inch fruit. Easily grown in containers or in the garden. Seed source: LED TOMA WILL

Specialized Mexican/ Southwestern Tomato Varieties

Zapotec Ribbed: An indeterminate, ruffled, Mexican tomato. The fruit weighs 2 to 4 pounds at maturity. Seed source: SEED

Mexican/Southwestern Herbs

Cilantro/Coriander

The leaf is called *cilantro*, and the seed is called *coriander*.

Long Standing: Seed source: BOU BURR COO COM GAR GUR HIG JLH NIC PIN RED RIC SEE SEED SOU VER

Mexican Coriander: The leaves on this variety are tough, but dry well. It is native to Central America. Seed source: RIC

Cumin

Ground cumin is used in many Mexican dishes, including chili. Cumin needs a long warm growing season.

Seed source: ABU BOU COM DEG GOU JLH LEJ NIC ORN PAR POR RED RIC SEE SOU VER WILL

Epazote

This herb is also called Mexican Tea, Goosefoot, or American Wormseed. The plant grows 24 to 48 inches tall. The fresh leaves are crushed, or dried and ground.

Seed source: ABU JLH JOH NIC ORN PIN PLA RED RIC SEE SEED SHE SOU TAY

Oregano

Mexican Oregano: A tender perennial with a fine flavor that Mexican cooks use extensively in a wide variety of dishes. Seed source: DAB RIC SEE TAY

Tarragon

Sweet Mace: Also called Sweet Marigold or Mexican Tarragon. Has narrow, glossy green, serrated, anise-flavored leaves. It can be grown in a container or tucked into the corner of the kitchen garden. Seed source: DAB RED SEED TAY

Chapter Ten

The French Kitchen Garden

The French make every meal a celebration. They insist on absolutely fresh vegetables to complement the fresh meats and fish they serve with delicious sauces. Salads created with a combination of greens tossed with a tart dressing can also be the highlight of a good French meal. French vegetables such as Touchon carrots and Vert de Massey *concombres* (cucumbers) have also become popular with American cooks who are looking for something different and authentic for their own French cooking.

French cooking isn't always the fancy cooking that Americans have become accustomed to. But the French always make the most of their vegetables; they don't simply add butter to them and serve them as a side dish. Broccoli, for instance, might be sprinkled with cheese and browned lightly, or potatoes might be sautéed with onions, red or green peppers, and herbs. They might serve stewed green tomatoes, add potato puree to cod, or serve eggplant puree with tomato that is lightly flecked with tarragon.

French vegetable varieties are currently becoming easier to find in this country, and every seed catalog will have some of them. We encourage every kitchen gardener to plant a few. We will also include a few select northern European varieties in this chapter. Bon appétit!

Artichokes (Artichauts)

Artichokes have a nutty flavor that makes them a favorite of good cooks. The artichoke has always been considered a gourmet vegetable by French chefs, who often braise artichokes in wine or sauté them in olive oil with herbs. Here's a French variety you should try.

Imperial Star: A new artichoke variety with a mild, sweet flavor and tender texture. Seed source: SHE

Beans (Haricots)

Green Beans (Haricots Verts)

French green beans are described as either gourmet types (*filets*) or commercial types (*mangetout*). *Filets* are as slim as a pencil and especially tender and tasty. A favorite way to serve them is as green beans with tomatoes and herbs (*haricots verts a la privebcake*). Another is to sauté them with olive oil and garlic and sprinkle them with bread crumbs (*haricots verts frais a l'ail*). Here are some varieties to try.

Emerite: A long, pencil-slim, *filet* pole green bean. The slim, round, fleshy, 7- to 9-inch pods have a crisp, brittle snap and a delicate flavor. Seed source: COU GOU ORN PIN SHE STO

Flageolet: A French heirloom variety used as a dry soup bean. Pure white seed. Seed source: COO ORG PIN SHE

Flambeau: Long, slender pod produces beans that are mint green. Seed source: JOH NIC

French Dwarf Horticultural: The long, straight pods grow on 14- to 18-inch plants. Use this variety as a green bean, or let it dry. Seed source: ALL COM

Vernandon: A true French *filet* bush green bean with long, round, pencil-slim, straight 5-inch pods. Vernandon is a full-flavored bean. Seed source: ORN SHE

Yellow Beans

Kinghorn: Also called Brittle Wax. This white, seeded French variety (nove) develops 5- to 6-inch creamy yellow pods. Seed source: GUR HIG SEE WILL

Rocd'or: Also called Rocdor, Roc D'Or. A bush variety with long, straight, round, yellow pods. Rocd'or has a light, delicate, buttery flavor.

Seed source: **GAR JOH NIC ORN SEED SHE**

Beets (Betteraves)

When picked small, beets can be extremely tasty. Boil or bake them in their skins, and serve them with a vinaigrette. The varieties included here are European.

Bolthardy: A deep red Dutch variety that has stringless sweet flesh. Seed source: THO

Kleine Bol: Also called Little Ball. This is a sweet-flavored Dutch baby beet. Extremely tender. Seed source: BURP HIG ORN PAR PIN SEE SHE STO TER TIL TWI WILL

Carrots (Carotes)

Some of the best tasting carrots are French varieties. Most are full flavored and nonfibrous. Included are some European varieties to try.

Amsdor: A new French hybrid, Amsterdam forcing/Nantes cross. Amsdors are beautiful, smooth, perfectly round carrots with deep orange flesh and a sweet full flavor. Seed source: SHE

Bolero Hybrid Nantes: These are slender, sweet, crunchy carrots. Seed source: SHE

Coreless Amsterdam: A Dutch Nantes variety that grows 6 to 7 inches long. Seed source: STO

Parmex: A round French forcing carrot. Grows well in shallow soil. Seed source: HIG ORN

Primo: An easy to pick, French variety with no green shoulders. You can serve this one as a baby carrot. Seed source: HIG

Chard

The French love chard, and you can find it piled high in French market stalls. The variety we recommend here is milder and sweeter than most American varieties. The stalks have a crunchy quality.

Paros: French variety with dark green, crinkled leaves. Seed source: SHE

Cress (Cresson)

In France, green grocers mix sprigs of cress with freshly cut lettuce.

Cresson: Also called Curly Cress. This French cress is ready to eat in

about 2 weeks. It is a favorite in northern France, where it grows well in cold weather. Seed source: SHE

Chicory (Chicorée)

French escarole and curly endive (*frisée*) both are prized for the crunchy texture and mild flavors.

Sinco: An escarole. Sinco produces a big head with crispy leaves folded around a crunchy heart. You can find this one in the market stalls of France. Seed source: SHE

Très Fine: A curled endive. Frilly leaves with crisp ribs and cream-colored hearts. Très Fine is a specialty of fine restaurants. Seed source: GOU HIG SHE

Leeks (Poireau)

Leeks are considered a gourmet "onion" in France. Leeks are delicious in soups or in a vinaigrette with marinated mushrooms.

Blue Solaize: A French heirloom variety that turns violet during autumn. Seed source: COO ORN SEE

Furor: A long, white-shaft, French variety. Seed source: ORN

Otina: This French variety has long, thick stems. Can also be used as a baby leek. Seed source: SHE

Tenor: Deep blue green leaves, 2 feet tall. French variety. Seed source: ORN SEE WIL

Vernor: A Blue Solaize French variety. Seed source: ORN

Cabbage (Chou)

You find cabbage grown in gardens all over Europe. It is stuffed, shredded for cole slaw, fried, stir-fried, or boiled.

Grenadier: This is a 3- to 5-pound Dutch variety with 8-inch heads. Crunchy, with a delicate, mild flavor. Seed source: SHE STO

Marner Alfroh: A German variety that produces a compact 3-pound round head. Seed source: BOU

Promasa: A baby savory cabbage. A small 1- to 2-pound cabbage that makes individual servings. It has crinkled blue green leaves. Seed source: NIC SHE TER

Cucumbers (Concombres)

Often cucumbers and tomatoes are served together garnished with watercress, or they are sliced into rounds and tossed with salt, wine vinegar, and sugar.

Cornichons De Bourbonne: This French variety is slightly curved and needs frequent harvesting. This is known as the "mini" pickle cucumber. Traditionally, cornichons are made into tiny, tangy, pickles. Seed source: **ORN SHE**

Long White: European variety that is white inside and out. Seed source: **ORN**

Vert De Massy: French cornichon type grows to 4 inches long. Seed source: **COO GOU HIG JOH NIC SEE**

Eggplant (Aubergines)

Cream-fleshed eggplants are used extensively in French cuisine. There are many ways to use eggplants. Garnish eggplant halves with fresh tomato and herbs (*Aubergines au Four, a La Provencale*), sauté eggplant with oil and garlic, or puree it (*Caviar d'aubergines*).

Debarentane: Named for the town, Debarentane, in France. Very elongated fruit. Seed source: **SEE**

Prelane: 7- to 9-inch-long, violet black French variety. Seed source: **NIC SHE**

Vernal: This French variety produces elongated teardrop-shaped, 10-ounce, shiny black fruit. Seed source: **GOU**

Lettuce (Laitue)

The French grow a wide variety of lettuces, although butterhead lettuce is preferred in France and most of Europe. *Mâche* (a mixture of exotic greens) is very popular in restaurants.

Iceberg Lettuce

Iceberg lettuce has a solid head.

Batavia Bord Rouge: The crumpled, dark green leaves are tinged deep red. Bitter variety. Seed source: **PIN**

La Brilliante: This French cross of a crisp head type with butterhead tenderness has toothed, vibrantly green leaves. Seed source: **COO**

Red Grenoble: Light green leaves are tinted red. Seed source: **COO GOU SHE**

Reine Des Glaces: Deeply cut, lacy, green leaves. Seed source: COO ORN SEE

Butterhead Lettuce

Butterhead has fairly thick, buttery-flavored folded leaves.

Brune D'Hiver: Smooth, fan-shaped green leaves with bronzy red edges. French heirloom variety. Seed source: ABU COO HIG ORN SEE SOU

Divina: Thick, dark green, shiny leaves. Good French variety. Seed source: GOU

Juliet: Thick, green leaves overlaid with a burgundy blush. Seed source: SHE

Mantilla: This French variety has apple green leaves. Seed source: ORN SHE

Rougette Du Midi: French variety with bronze red leaves, needs lots of water. Seed source: COO ORN

Loose-leaf Lettuce

These are the cut-and-come-again lettuces. The more you cut the leaves, the more they grow back.

Curly Oakleaf: Sometimes called Feuille De Chene or Foglie Di Quercial. A cutting lettuce that will form a head if thinned. Seed source: COO

Mascara: Dutch variety with dark red, oak type leaves. Seed source: TER

Red Oak Leaf: Deeply indented crimson, cranberry, or burgundy leaves. This is a gourmet type lettuce. Seed source: ORN SEED SHE

Romaine Lettuce

Romaine has broad, oblong, clustered leaves.

Balloon: Tall, heat-tolerant French variety. Seed source: COO SEE

Craquante D'Avignon: Deep green leaves. A semiromaine type. Seed source: COO

Rouge D'Hiver: Bronze to deep red, broad, flat leaves. This French heirloom variety is a favorite of specialty growers. Seed source: COO JLH ORN SEE SEED SHE

Melons (Melons)

The French adore Charentais melons, which they say are the only melon worth eating. In some cases, French farmers pass the seeds to these melons down to their sons to ensure the quality of their melons. They have a delightful aroma and wonderful sweet flavor. American seed companies have sold heirloom Charentais varieties for years. Now they sell a number of improved hybrids.

Acor: Charentais type with aromatic, deep orange flesh. Seed source: ORN

Chaca: French variety that produces 3-pound melons with a small seed cavity and orange flesh. Seed source: NIC PIN POR

Charentais: The famous French variety. Produces $3^1/_2$-pound melons. Seed source: NIC ORG SEE

Flyer: Grapefruit-sized European variety Charentais type. Seed source: JOH

Pancha: 2-pound, 6-inch-long melon with deep orange flesh. French variety. Seed source: SHE

Savor: French Charentais type that produces a 2-pound melon with deep orange flesh. This melon does not slip easily off the vine when ripe. Harvest when the skin between the sutures turns straw colored and the aroma is strong. Seed source: JOH NIC ORN TWI

Verdantais: Charentais type with smooth skin. Seed source: SEE

Onions (Oignons)

Copra: Dutch variety for long storage. A yellowish bronze onion with heavy scales. Seed source: GAR JOH STO

Simione Red Bottle: Intense carmine-colored French variety. Seed source: GAR GOU

Peppers (Poivrons)

Most French and European chefs cook with Lamuyo type bells, which are much bigger and more elongated than the familiar blocky bells.

Belconi: Long pepper that varies from intense green to shiny red at maturity. French variety. Seed source: GOU

Cadice: Very long, crunchy pepper. They have sweet flesh, firm walls, and a high gloss. Seed source: SHE

Ori: This French variety sets its 7-by-$3^1/_2$-inch yellow peppers under stressful conditions. Seed source: TOMA

Vidi: Elongated 7-inch lobed bell pepper. Has thick walls that turn from glossy green to deep red at maturity. A French variety that is disease tolerant. Seed source: COO GOU PIN SHE TOMA

Potatoes (Pommes)

Potatoes are found in many recipes. Try them sautéed with onion, peppers, and herbs (*pommes de terre sautees a la catalane*) or sauteed with garlic and herbs (*pommes de terre sautees a l'ail*).

We have been unable to find a French variety of potato sold by American seed companies. We suggest you try these instead.

Early Baby Epicure: White-fleshed, white-skinned potatoes. The plant will grow baby potatoes in 60 to 65 days. Seed source: SHE

Pumpkins (Potirons)

Pumpkins have been appearing in French markets for centuries. They are often eaten like winter squash.

Rouge D'Etampes: Also called Cinderella. This is a large French heirloom variety that is deeply lobed and flattened on top. Seed source: BOU COM COO GOU SEE SEED SHE

Radishes (Radis)

The flesh of French radishes lends an extra zest to salads. The following varieties are especially tasty.

D'Avignon: 3- to 4-inch-long, $\frac{1}{2}$-inch-thick radish. Red tapering to a white point. Seed source: GAR JOH

Flamboyant: 3 inches long, red with white tip. Seed source: SHE

Flamivil: 3 inches long, intensely red with white tip. Seed source: HIG JOH

Fluo: French cylindrical red radish with white tip. Seed source: COO GOU HIG ORN PIN

Shallots (Échalotes)

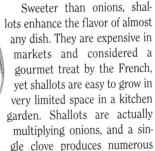

Sweeter than onions, shallots enhance the flavor of almost any dish. They are expensive in markets and considered a gourmet treat by the French, yet shallots are easy to grow in very limited space in a kitchen garden. Shallots are actually multiplying onions, and a single clove produces numerous bulbs. To grow, divide the shallot bulbs into cloves and plant the blunt end down just below the surface, 5 to 6 inches apart. Dig up as the foliage starts to collapse. Gray, frog-leg, and round French shallots are usually grouped together as red shallots.

Atlas: French-style shallot with brownish red skin and pinkish red flesh. Will grow almost anywhere. Seed source: JOH

French Shallot: Multiplies in soil. Seed source: GAR JOH NIC SOU VER WILL

Grey Shallot: Considered the true shallot in France. Seed source: LEJ

Pink Shallot: Large French variety. Vivid reddish pink skin and flesh. Seed source: SEE

Spinach (Epinard)

Europe produces some delicious spinach. It is often served in France with hard-boiled eggs (*a la tripe in lasagna*).

Nordic: Dutch variety that has vibrant, deep green leaves. Seed source: PAR SHE

Wolter: Dutch variety with almond-shaped, medium green leaves. Seed source: SHE

Tomatoes (Tomates)

In France and much of the European continent, growers stress the flavor and high quality of the fruit. This contrasts with some of the American varieties that often taste like cardboard when purchased from supermarkets. With most French cooking, the flavor is in the pulp. They generally get rid of the skin and the seeds. Try tomatoes baked with a topping of herbal crumbs (*tomates farcies a la provencal*).

Carmello: Large French variety that resists cracking. Indeterminate plant. Seed source: ORN SHE

Lorissa: Semideterminate plant. Deep red fruit. French variety. Seed source: ORN

Marmande: French variety. Semideterminate plant. Flat, scarlet red. Seed source: COO GOU ORN SEE TOMA WILL

Salsa: A round, red French variety. Seed source: TOMA

Turnips (Navets)

The French are partial to the young, sweet turnips sold in their farmers' markets. They are not nearly as strongly flavored as the American varieties. Harvest when small.

Di Milan: Harvest the white globe at 2 by 4 inches. Tops are rosy red. Pull them when they are small. They are often served with a light sauce. Seed source: GOU PIN SEE SHE

Zucchini (Courgettes)

In France, zucchini are bred for their tenderness. The blossoms of any of these zucchini can be sautéed, stuffed, or baked.

Arlesa: Pick while glossy green zucchini is less than 5 inches long. They stay firm and fresh after picking. Seed source: ORN SHE

French White Bush: 3 to 5 inches long. French variety. Seed source: NIC SEE

Ronde De Nice: Grows up to 6 inches in diameter. Round, pale green. French heirloom variety. Harvest them any time after they reach an inch in diameter. Stuff the larger ones. Seed source: BOU GOU SEED SHE

Chapter Eleven

Basic Kitchen Garden Vegetable Culture

Vegetables are divided by gardeners into warm-weather and cool-weather plants. Generally that means that some vegetables (primarily root and leaf crops) such as most greens, lettuce, cabbage, and broccoli grow well in temperatures ranging from 45° to 70°F. These are cool-season vegetables.

Most vegetables that produce fruit, beans, eggplant, peppers, and tomatoes grow best in temperatures ranging from 70° to 90°F. Many of the seeds, such as those of beans, won't germinate until the soil temperature warms to 65°F in the spring. Tomatoes won't set fruit until night temperatures stay above 55°F.

We are organic gardeners. We didn't start out to grow organic, but over the years, we have found it to be the most efficient way to garden. Today it's easier than ever before to garden organic. When we started, we had to combine our own nutrients to produce the mix of nitrogen, phosphorus, and potassium that we wanted. Today you can buy commercially mixed organic fertilizers in almost any formula you wish. In our culture section, we indicate the special needs of each vegetable.

While every garden will attract its share of insect pests and disease, we try not to get too upset about it. We strive to balance nature and use controls only when absolutely necessary. Over the years, we have developed an organic eight-step insect and disease plan that works for us.

Step 1.

Conduct regular fall and spring cleanups. Get rid of all weeds and refuse. Try to keep the garden clean, and place all garden waste, such as carrot tops, in the compost pile.

Step 2.

Plant your crops to avoid certain pests. In some areas, for instance, flea beetles are a problem in early spring. But because of the fleas' life cycle, vegetables planted three weeks later are hardly affected. Also, make it a regular practice to select varieties that are resistance to the most prevalent disease. For instance, we nearly always select tomato varieties marked "VFN." That means they are resistant to verticillium, fusarium wilt, and nematodes. A gardening neighbor or the county agricultural agent can alert you to the worst pests in your area for certain vegetables.

Step 3.

Rotate your vegetables in the bed. You can move them around even in a small bed. Tomatoes, for instance, should never be planted in the same spot two years in a row. This rule applies to almost all vegetables.

Step 4.

Encourage beneficial insects to inhabit your garden by planting pollen-rich plants. If your garden is bothered by aphids or white flies, consider using beneficial insects to control them. Lady bugs and lacewings, for instance, have a tremendous appetite for aphids. Trichogramma wasps will parasitize caterpillars. Many mail order firms offer beneficial insects. Peaceful Valley Farm Supply, PO Box 2200, Grass Valley, California 95945, offers a variety of beneficial insects and has a catalog that explains in some detail which beneficial insects control which insect pests.

Step 5.

Check your garden carefully every day for insects and disease. Pick off any beetles or caterpillars you see that you are certain are destroying your plants. Tomato hornworms can easily be spotted. Pick off and destroy them. Destroy any diseased leaves or branches you find. If an entire plant is infected, remove it from the garden.

Step 6.

Move to more direct controls if the damage becomes severe. Use yellow cardboard squares for white flies, try aluminum foil to repel aphids, use rolled up newspaper to trap insects. Use a hard spray from a hose to knock off aphids. Insecticidal soaps (such as Safer Soap) work as a smothering agent and can be applied up to the day of harvest. Mineral or vegetable oil products also serve to smother the insects without harming the plants. You can purchase all of these from any nursery or garden center.

Step 7.

For heavy infestation, use biological controls. Bt (*Bacillus thuringiensis*) is a bacterium that infects and kills most larvae (caterpillars). You can buy specific strains that attack individual pests such as mosquitoes. Milky spore disease attacks and kills Japanese beetle grubs in the soil.

Grasshopper bait, a predacious protozoa *Nosema locustae*, kills most species of grasshoppers. These biologicals are available from most nurseries and garden supply centers.

Step 8.

As a last resort, use botanical insecticides. Pyrethrin, an extract of the crushed dried flowers of *Chrysanthemum cinerariifolium*, a daisylike plant from Kenya, is used against a wide range of insects including ants, aphids, army worms, the Mexican bean beetle, cabbage loopers, harlequin bugs, and more. Rotenone comes from the Derris family of plants grown in the tropics. It is effective against many hard-to-kill insects such as the cucumber beetle and the harlequin bug.

In our culture section, which follows, we list the most prevalent pest and the best controls. This varies considerably from area to area. If you still have problems, try using our 8-step method.

Culture

This section is designed to give you the basic information you need to successfully plant a wide variety of vegetables and herbs in your garden. We are including a United Stated Department of Agriculture zone map (Figure 11-1). This will help you to find how hardy a particular vegetable is in your area and whether or not it will overwinter in your garden.

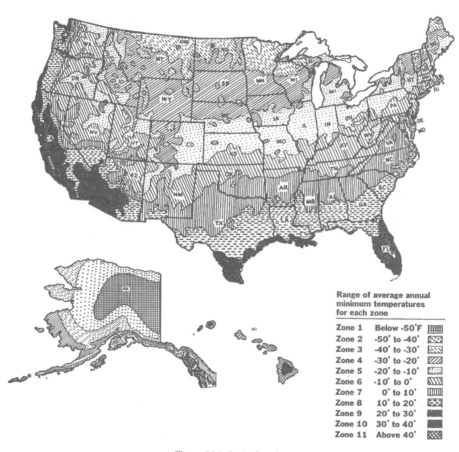

Figure 11-1. Agricultural zone map.

Vegetables

Artichokes (Cynara scolmus)

Sun/shade: Full sun to some shade.

Soil: Rich, moist, well drained; pH 6.4 to 7.5.

Planting: Start seed indoors in individual 4-inch pots and transplant outside 8 weeks later, after the soil has warmed up. One plant is enough for most kitchen gardens. When planting more than one, space 10 to 24 inches apart. Work 1 cup of organic fertilizer around each seedling. After the first year's harvest, remove the less vigorous plants, thinning to about 4 feet apart. Artichokes can also be started from young plants or divisions of old plants.

Nutrients: Feed in early spring and after harvest with one-quarter cup of complete organic fertilizer per plant.

Water: Keep the soil moist.

Hardiness: Hardy to zone 8. It will overwinter. Cover with straw to keep the stump from freezing out.

Pests/diseases: Mostly none.

Days to maturity: Seedlings will usually produce edible globes late in the first summer.

Asparagus (Asparagus officinalis)

Sun/shade: Full sun to shade.

Soil: Sandy loam; pH 6.0 to 8.0.

Planting: Start indoors in peat pots. After danger of frost has passed, set the plants out 10 to 24 inches apart in a 4-inch-deep furrow that you fill in as the plants grow.

Nutrients: Plant in a deep bed with lots of compost or manure. Feed in early spring and after harvest with 1 cup of organic fertilizer per 5-foot row.

Water: Keep uniformly moist.

Hardiness: Hardy to zone 4.

Pests/diseases: Asparagus beetles; control with rotenone. Rust, fusarium wilt, crown rot; avoid planting in old asparagus beds.

Days to maturity: Perennial. Asparagus can be harvested for 2 to 3 weeks the second year.

Beans, Pole (Phaseolus vulgaris)

Sun/shade: Full sun.

Soil: Average to rich garden soil; pH 6.0 to 7.5. Do not plant beans where other beans have grown in the past three years.

Planting: Sow the seed along the bottom of a trellis or support after the soil has warmed to 60°F. If you are planting to grow on poles, plant 5 to 6 seeds at the base of each pole. Plant $1^1/_2$ inches deep, 6 inches apart.

Nutrients: Beans draw the nitrogen for growth from the air with the help of soil bacteria. Feed plants every three to four weeks with fish emulsion, according to the instructions on the label.

Water: Avoid overhead watering.

Hardiness: No tolerance to frost, very tender.

Pests/diseases: Beans suffer from several diseases; keep water off the leaves. Mexican bean beetles and bean weevils; dust with rotenone.

Days to maturity: 65 to 90.

Beans, Bush (Phaseolus vulgaris)

Sun/shade: Grows well in full sun.

Soil: Needs average to rich garden soil; pH 6.0 to 7.5. Do not plant beans where other beans have grown in the past three years.

Planting: Plant bush beans $1^1/_2$ inches deep, 3 inches apart after the soil has warmed to 60°F. For a continuous harvest, make plantings every two weeks until mid-summer.

Nutrients: Use $^1/_2$ cup of complete organic fertilizer every 5 feet of row or its equivalent. Too much nitrogen causes poor pod set.

Water: Keep moist until the seeds germinate. Beans need to grow rapidly to maturity; do not let the soil dry out more than 3 or 4 inches deep.

Hardiness: Beans are quite tender.

Pests/diseases: Beans suffer from several diseases; keep water off the leaves. Mexican bean beetles and bean weevils; dust with rotenone.

Days to maturity: 45 to 60.

Beans, Lima (Phaseolus lunatus)

Sun/shade: Full sun.

Soil: Light, warm, and sandy; pH 6.0 to 7.5.

Planting: Plant after the soil has warmed up.

Nutrients: Lima beans supply their own nitrogen; feed every 3 to 4 weeks with a supplement organic fertilizer.

Water: Keep moist until the seed germinates. Don't allow the soil to crust over. Water deeply, and then don't water again until the soil dries out 3 to 4 inches deep.

Hardiness: Tender.

Pests/diseases: Aphids and Bean Leaf beetles; wash aphids off with a spray from a hose. Dust with rotenone.

Days to maturity: 70 to 95.

Bean, Dry, Shelling (Phaseolus vulgaris)

Sun/shade: Full sun.

Soil: Needs average to rich garden soil, well drained; pH 7.0 to 7.5.

Planting: Plant bush beans $1\frac{1}{2}$ inches deep, 3 inches apart after the soil has warmed up to 60 degrees F. For a continuous harvest, make plantings every two weeks until mid-summer. Pole beans plant $1\frac{1}{2}$ inches deep, 6 inches apart. Use supports for pole beans.

Nutrients: Use $\frac{1}{2}$ cup of complete organic fertilizer every 5 feet of row or its equivalent. Too much nitrogen causes poor pod set.

Water: Keep moist until the seeds germinate. Beans need to grow rapidly to maturity; do not let the soil dry out more than 3 or 4 inches deep.

Hardiness: Beans are quite tender.

Pests/diseases: Beans suffer from several diseases; keep water off the leaves. Mexican bean beetles and bean weevils; dust with rotenone.

Days to maturity: 90 to 125.

Beets (Beta vulgaris)

Sun/shade: Plant in full sun.

Soil: Light, loamy, and well drained; pH 6.0 to 7.5.

Planting: Sow beet seed across the planting bed $\frac{1}{2}$ inch deep and 1 inch apart. Tamp down. Beets can be sown in early spring for a summer crop. Sow in mid-summer for a fall crop. Beets can be planted in late fall in mild winter areas.

Nutrients: Mix in $\frac{1}{2}$ cup of organic fertilizer for every 2 square feet of beet bed, or every 5-foot row.

Water: Water overhead to keep both the tops and roots crisp. Water thoroughly in dry weather to prevent wilting. Don't let the soil dry out during root development.

Hardiness: Hardy. Beets can be planted in fall in mild winter areas.

Pests/diseases: Leaf miners can be a problem in some areas; pick and destroy the blistered leaves. Scab sometimes causes brown, rough spots on the skin; prevent this by keeping the soil near neutral: pH 7.0.

Days to maturity: 48 to 80.

Broccoli (Brassica oleracea Italica)

Sun/shade: Best in full sun.

Soil: Rich, heavy; pH 6.0 to 7.0.

Planting: Broccoli can be started indoors or in a hotbed two to three months before the last spring frost. Plant seedlings in the ground four to six weeks before the last frost. Broccoli does best when temperatures remain between 40° and 70°F over the growing season. Transplant in the ground 18 inches apart.

Nutrients: Broccoli is a heavy feeder. Put $1/4$ cup of organic fertilizer into the ground under each transplant. Feed once a month with fish emulsion, according to the instructions on the label.

Water: Never allow the roots to dry out. A light mulch will help keep the soil moist.

Hardiness: Hardy to zone 8.

Pests/diseases: Broccoli is affected by club root or cabbage root maggot; apply wood ashes around the stems of the plant. Imported cabbage worm eats holes in the leaves; control with Bt (*Bacillus thurigiensis*). Flea beetles chew tiny pinholes; spray with rotenone to keep the beetle population down. To foil cutworms, put paper cylinders around the seedlings.

Days to maturity: 65 to 70.

Brussels Sprouts (Brassica oleracea gemmifera)

Sun/shade: Full sun.

Soil: Almost any kind of soil is fine, although they don't like overly acidic conditions; pH 6.0 to 7.5.

Planting: Plant seed inside in peat pots 6 weeks before the last frost. Space on 24-inch centers.

Nutrients: Work $1/4$ cup of organic fertilizer into the ground under each transplant. Avoid excessive nitrogen.

Water: Never allow the roots to dry out. A light mulch will help keep the soil moist.

Hardiness: Very hardy.

Pests/diseases: Aphids; control with a hand spray. Control cabbage worms with Bt (*Bacillus thuringiensis*).

Days to maturity: 80 to 140.

Cabbage (Brassica oleracea capitata)

Sun/shade: Full sun is best.

Soil: Medium, light, and well drained; pH 6.0 to 7.5.

Planting: Start seed indoors 6 weeks before the last frost. Transplant to $2^1/_2$ feet apart. In mild winter areas, plant in fall or winter.

Nutrients: Cabbage is a heavy feeder. Work 1 cup of complete organic fertilizer into the soil around each plant.

Water: Never let the soil dry out. Mulch helps keep the soil moist and cool.

Hardiness: Most cabbages will withstand some frost.

Pests/diseases: Cabbage web worms; use Bt (*Bacillus thuringiensis*), and pick off the worms. Blackleg, spread by cutworms; collect and burn tops after harvest. Cover with row covers as a preventive measure. Practice crop rotation.

Days to maturity: 45 to 120.

Carrots (Daucus carota)

Sun/shade: Full sun to quarter shade.

Soil: Carrots like soil a bit on the sandy side. It should be deep, free of rocks, and well drained. Freshly manured soil can cause carrots to fork and split; pH 6.0 to 7.0.

Planting: Sow seeds across the bed and cover with $1/4$ inch of soil, vermiculite, or peat moss. Carrot seeds need to stay damp until they germinate. Thin to 1 to 2 inches apart.

Nutrients: Fertilize twice during the growing season with a complete organic fertilizer: $1/2$ cup per 2 square feet of space.

Water: Carrots need frequent watering. Don't allow to dry out.

Hardiness: Carrots are quite hardy.

Pests/diseases: Carrot rust fly; if this is a problem, prevent by using floating row covers or skip planting for a year to break the life cycle. Wireworms; sprinkle wood ashes in the bed.

Days to maturity: 50 to 110.

Cauliflower (Brassica oleracera botrytis)

Sun/shade: Full sun.

Soil: Light and rich; pH 6.0 to 7.5.

Planting: Start in peat pots about 6 weeks before the last frost. Space plants 18 to 24 inches apart. Plant in early spring or in summer for a fall crop.

Nutrients: Cauliflower is a heavy feeder. Mix $1/2$ cup of complete organic fertilizer into the soil around each plant.

Water: Always keep the soil moist. Cauliflower often needs extra water in dry weather.

Hardiness: Will withstand some frost to zone 8.

Pests/diseases: Cabbage webworm; apply Bt (*Bacillus thuringiensis*). Flea beetles can be a problem; control with rotenone.

Days to maturity: 30 to 180.

Celery (Apium graveolens dulce)

Sun/shade: Full sun for maximum development.

Soil: Rich, light, and sandy; pH 6.0 to 7.0.

Planting: Start inside in peat pots, and transplant outside 12 inches apart when the weather warms up. Celery actually does well as a spring or fall crop.

Nutrients: Fertilize well with a complete organic fertilizer.

Water: Keep well watered.

Hardiness: Fairly hardy. Should be covered with row cover when frost is expected.

Pests/diseases: The larva of the carrot fly can be an occasional pest. Earwigs can also be a pest.

Days to maturity: 60 to 140.

Celeriac (Apium graveolens rapaceum)

Sun/shade: Full sun for maximum root development.

Soil: Rich and well drained; pH 6.0 to 7.0.

Planting: Seedlings are rarely available from nurseries. Prepare a seed tray with planting mix, and sow seeds evenly. Water the surface, and then cover the tray with black plastic. When the seeds germinate, replace the black plastic with a clear plastic bag. Transplant into the garden when they are 3 to 4 inches high, 12 inches apart. You can also direct seed and place $^1/_2$ inch of soil over the seedbed. Keep moist until they sprout.

Nutrients: Celeriac needs lots of nitrogen. Use 1 tablespoon of blood meal mixed into 1 gallon of water.

Water: Water frequently, but don't saturate.

Hardiness: Quite hardy. Will tolerate frost.

Pests/diseases: Aphids; wash off with a hose.

Days to maturity: 110 to 120.

Chard, Swiss (Beta vulgaris cicla)

Sun/shade: Full sun to some shade.

Soil: Any well-drained soil; pH 6.0 to 7.5.

Planting: Sow seeds $^1/_2$ inch deep. When 3 to 5 inches high, thin to stand 8 to 10 inches apart.

Nutrients: Feed every 4 to 6 weeks with a complete organic fertilizer.

Water: Never let chard wilt. Mulch helps keep the soil moist.

Hardiness: Will withstand moderate cold and light frosts.

Pests/diseases: Snails can bother the plants; put out saucers of beer. Watch for signs of aphids; spray with an insecticidal soap. Leaf miners can also be a problem in some areas; pick and destroy the blistered leaves.

Days to maturity: 50 to 60.

Collards (Brassica oleracea acephala)
Sun/shade: Medium.

Soil: Light, well drained; pH 6.0 to 7.5.

Planting: Plant seed $1/2$ inch deep. When established, thin to stand 2 feet apart. Where winter temperatures rarely drop below 25°F, sow seeds in late summer to early fall.

Nutrients: Feed with a high-nitrogen organic fertilizer: $1/2$ cup per plant.

Water: Collard roots lie close to the surface; keep them moist.

Hardiness: This is a warm-weather plant and not take frost.

Pests/diseases: Few pests. Cabbage worms; control with Bt (*Bacillus thuringiensis*).

Days to maturity: 45 to 80.

Corn, Sweet (Zea mays)
Sun/shade: Full sun.

Soil: Sandy, somewhat fertile; pH 6.0 to 7.0.

Planting: Sow seeds 2 inches deep, 5 to 6 inches apart; thin to 10 to 12 inches apart. Sow in blocks to ensure pollination. Corn does not like cold, wet soils. Sow every two weeks until mid-summer for continuous harvest.

Nutrients: Corn needs nitrogen fertilizer during its early growth. Follow instructions on the package.

Water: Water the plants when they show any signs of wilting. Keep the ground moist when the tassels appear.

Hardiness: Seeds need a warm soil (65°F and above) in which to mature. Not cold-tolerant.

Pests/diseases: Corn earworm; apply one drop of mineral oil inside the silks at the tip of the ear. Corn borers; control with rotenone/pyrethrin. Corn smut forms large puffy, gray, irregular masses of fungus; pick off and destroy the fungus.

Days to maturity: 60 to 110.

Cucumbers (Cucumis sativus)
Sun/shade: Full sun to quarter shade.

Soil: Sandy to loam, with well-rotted manure or compost mixed in; pH 5.5 to 7.0.

Planting: Sow seeds $\frac{1}{2}$ inch deep. Space 6 to 10 inches apart. You can also sow 5 to 6 seeds per clump, $\frac{1}{2}$ inch deep. Space clumps 3 feet apart. Thin to the best 1 or 2 plants per clump. You can grow cucumbers up a wire or trellis to save space.

Nutrients: Fertilize about every 4 weeks with a heavy-nitrogen fertilizer. Mix $\frac{1}{2}$ cup of organic fertilizer in the soil around each plant.

Water: Keep the soil moist.

Hardiness: Intolerant of frost.

Pests/diseases: Sow bugs can be a problem with young plants; sprinkle with rotenone when you first set them out. Spotted cucumber beetle carries bacterial wilt; use rotenone. Powdery and downey mildew, which occur during hot, dry and wet, cool weather respectively; plant varieties resistant to mildew.

Days to maturity: 50 to 75.

Eggplant (Solanum melongena esculentum)

Sun/shade: Full sun to quarter shade.

Soil: Fertile, well drained, with decomposed manure added; pH 5.5 to 6.5.

Planting: Start seeds indoors. Place plants in the garden 18 inches apart when the nighttime lows are above 45°F. Low nighttime temperatures prevent fruit set.

Nutrients: Fertilize with an organic fertilizer low in nitrogen. Mix $\frac{1}{2}$ cup in the soil around each plant. Excess nitrogen results in all foliage and little fruit.

Water: Soak the soil deeply, but don't keep it saturated.

Hardiness: Very tender.

Pests/diseases: Aphids; spray underside of leaves with a hose. Flea beetles; control with pyrethrin.

Days to maturity: 53 to 125.

Garlic (Allium sativum)

Sun/shade: Full sun.

Soil: Rich, moist, well-drained soil; pH 6.0 to 7.5.

Planting: Prepare the garlic bed by mixing in compost and a complete organic fertilizer. Separate the cloves just before planting. Plant them 4 to 6 inches apart, and cover with 1 to 2 inches of soil.

Nutrients: During the growing season, fertilize with fish emulsion every few weeks according to the instructions on the label.

Water: Water every few days during dry weather. Water less frequently before harvesting.

Hardiness: Quite hardy. Recommended for zones 3 to 9.

Pests/diseases: Rotate the garlic bed to prevent the build-up of diseases.

Days to maturity: 8-11 months.

Horseradish (Ammoracia rusticana)
Sun/shade: Full sun to half shade.

Soil: Average to rich soil.

Planting: Start from a piece of root that has a green shoot.

Nutrients: Fertilize with a complete organic fertilizer.

Water: Keep well watered.

Hardiness: Very hardy to zone 4.

Pests/diseases: Few.

Days to maturity: 1 year.

Kale (Brassica oleraclea acephala)
Sun/shade: Full sun to half shade.

Soil: Likes rich soil that was manured for a previous crop.

Planting: Sow seeds $1/2$ inch deep; thin to 18 inches apart. You can often increase germination by covering with a fine layer of peat moss or vermiculite.

Nutrients: Feed every 3 to 4 weeks with fish emulsion.

Water: Water kale well in dry weather.

Hardiness: Very hardy. You can harvest from beneath the snow.

Pests/diseases: Aphids; knock off with a hose spray. Flea beetles; use rotenone.

Days to maturity: 47 to 75.

Kohlrabi (Brassica olerica)
Sun/shade: Full sun.

Soil: Fertile and loamy; pH 6.0 to 7.5.

Planting: Sow seeds in early spring as soon as the soil can be worked, $1/2$ inch deep and 2 to 3 inches apart. Thin to stand 3 to 4 inches apart. Make several plantings 2 weeks apart.

Nutrients: Feed with $1/2$ cup of complete organic fertilizer per 5 feet of row.

Water: Keep well watered.

Hardiness: Quite hardy.

Pests/diseases: Aphids.

Days to maturity: 49 to 70.

Leeks (Allium ampeloprasum porrum)
Sun/shade: Best in full sun.

Soil: Light, sandy to loam, and well manured; pH 6.0 to 8.0.

Planting: Leeks are a cool-season crop. Start the seed in a flat for transplanting into the garden. When transplanting, place the first leaves 4 to 6 inches below the soil level so that you have a good length of blanched stem. Space 6 inches apart. You can also directly sow the seed 1 to 2 inches apart. Cover with $^1/_2$ inch of soil or peat moss. You can fall blanch by piling straw around the base of the plants.

Nutrients: Work $^1/_2$ cup of organic fertilizer into the ground below the seeds or transplants. Feed every four weeks with fish emulsion.

Water: Water every day in dry weather.

Hardiness: Very hardy.

Pests/diseases: Onion maggot.

Days to maturity: 70 to 150.

Lettuce (Lactuca sativa)

Sun/shade: Lettuce does well in partial shade. Many of the lettuces do best when the air temperature is between 60° to 70°F.

Soil: Moist but well drained and mixed with well-rotted manure; pH 6.0 to 7.0.

Planting: Start planting lettuce as soon as the soil can be worked. Many varieties will germinate in soil temperatures as low as 40°F. Sow seeds $^1/_2$ inch deep across the bed. Thin to stand 6 to 12 inches apart. By selecting the right varieties, you can plant lettuce every three weeks during the summer season. For transplanting, sow seeds across a flat filled with potting mix. When the plants are about an inch high, transplant into individual pots. Plant them outside when they are 3 or 4 inches high.

Nutrients: Fertilize with a good organic fertilizer at planting time. Use 1 cup of complete organic fertilizer per 3 square feet of garden space.

Water: Keep moist, but not overly watered.

Hardiness: Lettuce will withstand light frosts.

Pests/diseases: Slugs can be a problem; control with diatomaceous earth. Aphids wash off with a strong spray of water. Lettuce can be damaged with stem rot.

Days to maturity: 45 to 100.

Melons (Cucumis melo)

Sun/shade: Full sun.

Soil: Light, sandy; pH 6.0 to 7.5.

Planting: Melon seeds require a minimum soil temperature of 60°F for germination. The optimum range for melon growth is between 65° and 85°F. Plant 2 or 3 seeds together, 1 to $1^{1}/_{2}$ inches deep. If grown up a trellis, space about 15 inches apart. When about 5 inches high, thin to leave the largest plant. You can also let a few melon plants take over a portion of a flower bed.

Nutrients: Use $^{1}/_{2}$ cup of a high-nitrogen organic fertilizer worked into the soil for each plant.

Water: Give them plenty of water early in the season, then water thoroughly in dry weather.

Hardiness: Very tender.

Pests/diseases: Sow bugs can be a problem for young seedlings; use rotenone. Cucumber beetle carries bacterial wilt; control the beetles with rotenone. Powdery mildew; control by planting resistant varieties. Once the leaves become mildewed, the unripe melons will rot.

Days to maturity: 70 to 120.

Mustard (Brassica juncea)

Sun/shade: Full sun to half shade.

Soil: Rich, mixed with rotted manure; pH 6.0 to 7.5.

Planting: Sow seeds across bed, and cover with $^{1}/_{2}$ inch of soil and vermiculite. Thin to stand 6 to 8 inches apart.

Nutrients: Use only rotted manure in the soil.

Water: Water regularly.

Hardiness: Fairly hardy.

Pests/diseases: Aphids, wash off with water spray. Cabbage looper, imported cabbage worm, control with BT.

Days to maturity: 35 to 85.

Okra (Hibiscus esculentus)

Sun/shade: Full sun.

Soil: Rich and loamy; pH 6.0 to 8.0.

Planting: Sow seeds indoors in containers, about a month before planting outside. Soak the seeds in water 24 hours before planting. Many nurseries carry transplants. Space 18 inches apart. You can direct seed into the bed when the soil warms up.

Nutrients: Fertilize twice during the growing season with fish emulsion, or use $^{1}/_{2}$ cup of complete fertilizer per plant.

Water: Keep moist but don't overwater.

Hardiness: Will not tolerate frost.

Pests/diseases: Corn earworm; control with Ryania.

Days to maturity: 45 to 90.

Onions (Allium cepa)

Sun/shade: Full sun.

Soil: Firm, sandy to loam, fertile; add generous amounts of organic matter; pH 5.5 to 7.0.

Planting: It is easiest to start from sets (small bulbs are available at most nurseries) in mid-spring. Set 1 to 2 inches deep, and space 2 to 3 inches apart. Sow the seeds across the bed. Thin to stand 2 to 3 inches apart. Thin scallions $1/2$ inch apart.

Nutrients: Apply $1/2$ cup of nitrogen-rich organic fertilizer for each 2 square feet of onion bed, or each 5-foot row.

Water: Water steadily; keep the soil moisture high in the top 8 to 12 inches of soil.

Hardiness: Fairly hardy.

Pests/diseases: Onion maggot; bacterial soft rot. Rotate onions each year, practice garden cleanliness.

Days to maturity: 95 to 150.

Parsnips (Pastinaca sativa)

Sun/shade: Full sun to partial shade.

Soil: Rich, recently manured soil. Cultivate the bed to a depth of at least 18 inches and remove all rocks.

Planting: Sow seeds in spring as soon as the ground can be worked, about 1 inch apart. Cover with $1/2$ inch of soil or vermiculite. Thin to stand 3 to 6 inches apart.

Nutrients: Fresh manure or nitrogen fertilizer causes the roots to fork.

Water: Water regularly while the roots are small.

Hardiness: Will overwinter where the temperature stays above 25°F.

Pests/diseases: Carrot rust fly maggots can injure the roots; control by using crop row covers.

Days to maturity: 94 to 145.

Peas (Pisum sativum)

Sun/shade: Full sun.

Soil: Rich and recently manured; pH 6.0 to 7.5.

Planting: Start peas in the spring as soon as the soil can be worked. Plant 1 inch deep and 2 to 3 inches apart. Support pea vines on a trellis or fence. Do not thin the plants.

Nutrients: Work in 1 pound of bone meal for every 10 square feet of bed.

Water: Peas need plenty of water.

Hardiness: Extremely hardy.

Pests/diseases: Damping off and downy mildew; use a biological fungicide.

Copper sulfate (a mineral organic fungicide) controls downy mildew. Pea aphid; use pyrethrin.

Days to maturity: 57 to 100.

Peppers, Sweet (Capsicum frutescens) *and Peppers, Hot* (C. annuum)

Sun/shade: Full sun.

Soil: Rich, well-drained loam; pH 5.5 to 7.0.

Planting: Start indoors in the spring 6 to 8 weeks before nighttime temperatures stay above 55°F. Transplant them out when the soil temperatures have warmed to 60° to 65°F. Space 18 to 24 inches apart.

Nutrients: Fertilize with a low-nitrogen organic fertilizer; mix $^1/_2$ cup around each plant. Excess nitrogen produces a bushy plant with little fruit. Bone meal helps get the plants off to a fast start.

Water: Provide an even water supply. Drip irrigation works well for peppers.

Hardiness: Tender.

Pests/diseases: Cutworms; use a cardboard collar sunk into the soil. A floating row cover used early in the season eliminates many insect problems.

Days to maturity: 45 to 86.

Potatoes (Solanum tuberosum)

Sun/shade: Full sun to quarter shade.

Soil: Light and sandy to loam, with generous amounts of manure or other organic materials, plus phosphorus and potash. Spade thoroughly; pH 4.8 to 6.5.

Planting: Cut the seed potatoes into squares with one good eye per piece. Place the pieces with the cut side down, 4 inches deep, 12 inches apart.

Nutrients: Add phosphorus and potash to the soil. Fertilize with organic nitrogen when the plants are about 6 inches high.

Water: Water regularly, but don't saturate the soil. The crop needs water if the newly developing leaves have a bluish tinge.

Hardiness: The leaves are susceptible to frost, but they will come back.

Pests/diseases: Flea beetles and Colorado potato beetle; control with pyrethrum.

Days to maturity: 70 to 120.

Pumpkins (Cucurbita pepo)

Sun/shade: Full sun.

Soil: Rich, well manured; pH 5.5 to 7.5.

Planting: Plant pumpkin seeds outdoors when the nighttime temperature stays above 55°F. Plant seeds directly into the ground.

Nutrients: Use $\frac{1}{2}$ cup of a complete organic fertilizer dug in around the plant. Apply another $\frac{1}{2}$ cup as the plants begin to vine.

Water: Do not cover the crowns with water or keep the soil continuously moist. Mulch to conserve moisture.

Hardiness: Tender; plant only after the soil has warmed up. Optimum soil temperature for germination is 70° to 90°F.

Pests/diseases: Vine borers, squash bugs, and spotted cucumber beetle, which carries bacterial wilt. Sow bugs often attack young plants; use rotenone.

Days to maturity: 75 to 120.

Radishes (Raphanus sativus)

Sun/shade: Full sun to partial shade.

Soil: Mix in ample well-rotted manure; pH 6.0 to 7.0.

Planting: Radishes can be grown from early spring to late fall. Sow across the bed, and thin to stand 1 to 2 inches apart.

Nutrients: Add an organic fertilizer before planting.

Water: Radishes have shallow root systems; keep the soil moist.

Hardiness: Very hardy.

Pests/diseases: Flea beetle (leaves are shot through with tiny holes); use rotenone or a combination of rotenone/pyrethrum spray.

Days to maturity: 21 to 150.

Rhubarb (Rheum rhaponticum)

Sun/shade: Full sun to partial shade.

Soil: Deep, rich, and slightly acid; pH 5.5 to 7.0.

Planting: Plant the crowns in early spring, 1 to 2 feet apart. Makes an attractive plant in the flower bed. You can also start the plants from seeds indoors. Transplant after 3 to 4 weeks of growth.

Nutrients: Work bone meal and potash into the root area.

Water: Give rhubarb plenty of water.

Hardiness: Very hardy.

Pests/diseases: Few.

Days to maturity: Harvest rhubarb the second year.

Rutabagas (Brassica napobrassica)

Sun/shade: Full sun.

Soil: Light, sandy to loam; pH 5.5 to 7.0.

Planting: Sow seeds across the bed 3 to 4 inches apart. Cover with $\frac{1}{2}$ inch of soil or vermiculite. Space 8 to 12 inches apart.

Nutrients: Feed the plants with an application of organic nitrogen fertilizer: $\frac{1}{2}$ cup per 10 square feet.

Water: Mulch to prevent drying out.

Hardiness: Very hardy.

Pests/diseases: Few.

Days to maturity: 80 to 95.

Salsify (Tragopogon porrifolius)

Sun/shade: Full sun.

Soil: Deep, rich loam, with no manure or stones.

Planting: Sow the seeds across the bed, cover with 1 inch of soil, and thin plants to stand 3 inches apart.

Nutrients: Add $\frac{1}{2}$ cup of organic fertilizer per 10 square feet of bed.

Water: Keep well watered.

Hardiness: Hardy.

Pests/diseases: Root maggots, control by using row covers.

Days to maturity: 120 to 150.

Spinach (Spinacia oleracea)

Sun/shade: Full sun to partial shade.

Soil: Light, thoroughly worked, with plenty of organic matter added; pH 6.0 to 7.5.

Planting: Sow seeds across the bed, and cover with 1 inch of soil or vermiculite. Thin to stand 6 inches apart.

Nutrients: Use $\frac{1}{2}$ cup of blood meal per 5 square feet of garden space.

Water: Spinach needs plenty of water. However, spinach does not do well in poorly drained soil.

Hardiness: Reasonably hardy.

Pests/diseases: Spinach leaf miners (you can spot them by the blotchy trails on the leaves); destroy affected leaves.

Days to maturity: 40 to 79.

Squash, Summer (Cucurbita pepo)

Sun/shade: Full sun.

Soil: Very rich and well manured; pH 6.0 to 7.5.

Planting: Plant squash seeds outdoors when the nighttime temperatures have risen to 55°F. Plant seeds directly in the ground.

Nutrients: Use $\frac{1}{2}$ cup of a complete organic fertilizer dug in around the plant.

Apply another $^1/_2$ cup as the plants begin to vine.

Water: Mulch to conserve water.

Hardiness: Tender; plant only after the soil has warmed up. Optimum soil temperature for germination is 70° to 90°F.

Pests/diseases: Vine borers, squash bugs, and spotted cucumber beetle, which carries bacterial wilt. Sow bugs often attack young plants; use rotenone.

Days to maturity: 75 to 120.

Squash, Winter (Cucurbita maxima and C. moschata)

Sun/shade: Full sun.

Soil: Rich and well manured; pH 6.0 to 7.5.

Planting: Plant seeds outdoors when the nighttime temperatures have risen to 55°F. Plant seeds directly in the ground.

Nutrients: Use $^1/_2$ cup of a complete organic fertilizer dug in around the plant. Apply another $^1/_2$ cup as the plants begin to vine.

Water: Mulch to conserve water.

Hardiness: Tender; plant only after the soil has warmed up. Optimum soil temperature for germination is 70° to 90°F.

Pests/diseases: Vine borers, squash bugs, and spotted cucumber beetle, which carries bacterial wilt. Sow bugs often attack young plants; use rotenone.

Days to maturity: 75 to 120.

Sweet Potatoes (Ipomoea batatas)

Sun/shade: Full sun.

Soil: Light, sandy, and shallow; pH 5.5 to 6.5.

Planting: Plant sweet potato slips in the spring, 9 to 12 inches apart.

Nutrients: This vegetable does well with light fertilization.

Water: Can tolerate dry soil once it's established.

Hardiness: Tender.

Pests/diseases: Sweet potato weevil, pick off or use rotenone.

Days to maturity: 90 to 150.

Tomatoes (Lycopersicon esculentum)

Sun/shade: Full sun.

Soil: Enrich the bed with well-rotted manure or garden compost and dig deeply; pH 5.5 to 7.5.

Planting: Plant indoors 6 to 8 weeks before the last spring frost. Seeds germinate best in a temperature range of 70° to 90°F. If the tomatoes have become leggy, plant them deep and the stems will sprout roots. Space determinate varieties 18 to 24 inches apart; space indeterminate varieties 36 inches apart. Use a tomato cage around indeterminate varieties. Tomatoes need a nighttime temperature of above 55°F to set fruit.

Nutrients: Work $1/4$ cup of organic fertilizer into the ground around each plant. Feed with fish emulsion as the fruit begins to set. Follow the instructions on the label.

Water: Water regularly. Mulch to ensure an even moisture content.

Hardiness: Tender. Indeterminate varieties will produce fruit until the first hard frost.

Pests/diseases: Tomato hornworm; use Bt (*Bacillus thuringiensis*). Verticillium and fusarium wilt; plant disease-resistant varieties.

Days to maturity: 50 to 100.

Turnips (Brassica rapa)

Sun/shade: Full sun.

Soil: Loamy soils; avoid fresh manure; pH 5.5 to 7.0.

Planting: Sow seed across the bed 4 to 6 weeks before the last frost. Cover with $1/2$ inch of soil or vermiculite. Thin to 2 to 4 inches apart.

Nutrients: Fertilize with $1/2$ cup of light-nitrogen organic fertilizer per 5 square feet of bed or per each 10 foot row.

Water: Keep well watered.

Hardiness: Hardy.

Pests/diseases: Protect from root maggots by using floating row covers. Flea beetle attack; use rotenone.

Days to maturity: 28 to 80.

Herbs

Growing herbs is not much different from growing vegetables. In fact, in some cases it is much easier. Herbs can often survive in dry locations in very poor soil, although they will do best if you give them well-drained loam fortified with compost and manures.

Anise, basil, chervil, coriander, dill, sweet fennel, summer savory, parsley, chives, thyme, and winter savory are grown as annuals; borage, marjoram, oregano, mint, sage, rosemary, and tarragon are grown as perennials. In most case, you don't have to pull the entire plant to harvest it; you simply prune it by clipping the leaves.

Anise Hyssop (Agastache foeniculum)

Use the petals in salads and soups, and as flavoring for meat and desserts.

Sun/shade: Full to half sun.

Soil: Average soil.

Planting: Can be planted from both seeds and plants.

Nutrients: Not fussy.

Water: Water only in dry periods.

Hardiness: Fairly hardy. Withstands most frost.

Pests/diseases: None.

Annual/perennial: Perennial; plants will flower the first year from seeding in March.

Balm, Lemon (Melissa officianalis)

Use as lemon flavoring for tea and desserts.

Sun/shade: Full sun to shade.

Soil: Needs average soil.

Planting: Start from seedlings. Will spread from seeds.

Nutrients: Doesn't need fertilizer.

Water: Tolerates some dryness.

Hardiness: Tolerant to some frost.

Pests/diseases: None.

Annual/perennial: Perennial.

Basil (Ocimun spp.)

The number-one culinary herb. Good cooks can't do without it.

Sun/shade: Full sun.

Soil: Soil rich in organic material.

Planting: Sow seed in the spring when the ground has warmed up. Plant seeds $1/8$ inch deep, and thin to 1 foot apart. Space seedlings 1 foot apart. Basil grows from 6 inches to 2 feet tall depending on the variety planted.

Nutrients: Likes fish emulsion about every 6 weeks.

Water: Water regularly.

Hardiness: Tender; will not withstand frost.

Pests/diseases: Sow bugs; use rotenone.

Annual/perennial: Annual.

Bee Balm (Monarda didyma)

Use the flowers in salads and tea.

Sun/shade: Full sun to half shade.

Soil: Average soil.

Planting: Space 6 to 8 inches apart.

Nutrients: One feeding of fish emulsion.

Water: Keep moist.

Hardiness: Fairly hardy.

Pests/diseases: Mildew. Don't water leaves.

Annual/perennial: Perennial.

Borage (Borage officinalis)

Borage has bristly, gray green leaves and star-shaped bright blue flowers. The sprouts and first set of leaves have a cucumber flavor. Excellent for salads.

Sun/shade: Full sun to three-quarter shade.

Soil: Any soil.

Planting: Sow seeds outdoors in the fall or very early spring. Barely cover with soil. Borage can be easily grown in pots indoors; just place the pot in a sunny location and keep moist. Give the roots plenty of growing room. Borage will drop seeds every year, and new plants will come up the next spring. Borage grows 2 to 3 feet tall. When seedlings are about 2 inches high, space them 1 to 2 feet apart. To obtain a hedgelike border, space one foot apart.

Nutrients: Once or twice a year with fish emulsion.

Water: Keep moist. Needs only moderate amounts.

Hardiness: Tender.

Pests/diseases: Few.
Annual/perennial: Annual.

Chamomile, German (Matricania recutita)

Produces white daisylike flowers that bloom most of the summer. Makes a refreshing tea.

Sun/shade: Full sun to half shade.

Soil: Average; will grow in dry soil.

Planting: Buy seeds, and start in pots. Do not cover seed; it needs light to germinate. Transplant when they are about 6 inches high. Space about 6 inches apart. Grows to a height of 8 inches. You can also start from sets.

Nutrients: Use fish emulsion 2 or 3 times a year.

Water: Plants will grow in dry soil. Moist soil produces a dense mat of plant.

Hardiness: Moderately hardy.

Pests/diseases: Few.

Annual/perennial: Annual.

Chervil (Anthriscus cereifolium)

Chervil has light green, fernlike leaves that resemble parsley. It produces tiny umbrellalike clusters and flowers. The leaves and seeds have a delicate licorice flavor.

Sun/shade: It doesn't like full shade. Grow in filtered sun.

Soil: Will grow in average soil.

Planting: Sow seeds in place in early spring, or buy plants from nursery. Chervil grows to 2 feet tall. Chervil will reseed itself.

Nutrients: Feed occasionally with fish emulsion.

Water: Water regularly.

Hardiness: Very hardy. It will overwinter in mild winter climates.

Pests/diseases: Leaf miners can be a problem; grow under a floating row cover.

Annual/perennial: Annual.

Chives (Allium schoenoprasum)

A favorite herb, chives have hollow, grasslike leaves and love continuous clipping. If not clipped, chives will produce lavender flower heads that can be used in cooking or for decoration. There are many recipes that call for chives.

Sun/shade: Productive in full sun, but will grow well in partial shade.

Soil: Likes rich soil.

Planting: Start from plants or from

seed. You can also divide chives in early spring. In hot summer areas where temperatures remain over 90°F for prolonged periods, plant the root clumps in late summer or fall. Set root clumps 2 inches deep, 5 to 6 inches apart. Plant seeds $1/2$ inch deep; thin seedlings to 6 inches apart.

Nutrients: Start with $1/2$ cup of nitrogen-rich, organic fertilizer per clump.

Water: Water frequently. Don't let the soil dry out.

Hardiness: Fairly hardy.

Pests/diseases: Few.

Annual/perennial: Perennial.

Cilantro/Coriander (Coriandrum sativum)

Cilantro has delicate, fernlike leaves and pinkish white flowers. The seeds (coriander) turn from green to brown when they ripen. The leaves are extremely fragrant, but are often an acquired taste. This plant and its seeds are used in both Oriental and Mexican dishes.

Sun/shade: Full sun to three-quarter shade.

Soil: Average to rich.

Planting: Sow in place in early spring after danger of frost has passed. Also sow in the fall in mild winter areas. Seed is slow to germinate. After that, coriander reseeds itself every year. Sow seeds $3/4$ inch deep when the seedlings are about 2 inches high; thin to 8 to 10 inches apart. Coriander grows to 3 feet.

Nutrients: Feed with nitrogen-rich organic fertilizer.

Water: Water frequently, and keep the soil moist for good leaf production.

Hardiness: Seeds will overwinter in mild winter areas.

Pests/diseases: Almost none.

Annual/perennial: Annual.

Dill (Anethum graveolens)

Dill has lacy, light-green leaves and grows to a height of 2 to 4 feet. It has tiny, greenish yellow flowers in umbrellalike clusters. This plant sets itself apart in any garden. The leaves and seeds are used extensively in cooking.

Sun/shade: Full sun.

Soil: Likes rich soil, but will survive in poor soil.

Planting: Start from seed. Sow in the spring or in the fall before the ground freezes over. It will often reseed from year to year.

Nutrients: Fertilize with fish emulsion according to the instructions on the label.

Water: Keep watered.

Hardiness: Not hardy.

Pests/diseases: Aphids; use a hard spray of water to control.

Annual/perennial: Annual.

Fennel (Foeniculum vulgare)

Fennel is similar to dill, with yellow green, finely cut leaves. The yellow flowers grow in clusters.

Sun/shade: Full sun.

Soil: Likes average to rich soil.

Planting: Start from seed or plants. Barely cover the seeds with soil. When seedlings are about 2 inches high, thin to 12 inches apart. Fennel grows to 4 feet tall.

Nutrients: Use fish emulsion according to the directions on the label.

Water: Keep the soil moist.

Hardiness: Fairly hardy. Will survive in warm winter areas.

Pests/diseases: Few.

Annual/perennial: Perennial.

Hyssop (Hyssopus officinalis)

An 18-inch-high, shrublike herb with narrow, dark green, pungent (piney) leaves. Produces spikes of dark blue flowers.

Sun/shade: Full sun.

Soil: Will grow in average soil.

Planting: Best if started from plants. Seeds are available. Sow seeds in the spring or propagate by cuttings or divisions in the spring or fall. Sow seeds $1/4$ inch deep, 1 foot apart.

Nutrients: Feed occasionally with fish emulsion.

Water: Water only occasionally.

Hardiness: Fairly hardy.

Pests/diseases: Few.

Annual/perennial: Perennial.

Lemon Grass (Cymbopogon citratus)

Lemon Grass grows 1 foot high and produces grasslike leaves. It is used extensively in Asian cuisine.

Sun/shade: Full sun to half shade.

Soil: Average to rich; add compost.

Planting: Sow seeds in late fall or early spring. You can also grow by layering, by division in the spring, or by cuttings taken in the spring or summer. Plant 2 feet apart.

Nutrients: Feed with fish emulsion.
Water: Keep watered.
Hardiness: Very tender.
Pests/diseases: Few.
Annual/perennial: Perennial.

Lovage (Levisticum officinale)

Lovage produces deep green, divided leaves with clusters of small, greenish yellow flowers. Lovage has a celerylike flavor; use it in soups, stocks, stews, and sauces.

Sun/shade: Full sun to half shade.
Soil: Rich.
Planting: Start from seeds or plants. Divide old plants. Sow seeds in the spring after the night temperatures rise above 40°F. Lovage seed can also be sown in early fall. Sow seeds $^1/_4$ inch deep, 2 to 3 feet apart.
Nutrients: Feed with fish emulsion.
Water: Keep moist.
Hardiness: Very hardy.
Pests/diseases: Leaves sometimes attacked by leaf miners; remove and destroy damaged leaves.
Annual/perennial: Perennial.

Marjoram, Sweet (Origanum majorana)

This herb has small, oval, gray green leaves and spikes of white flowers. Sweet marjoram is an outstanding culinary herb.

Sun/shade: Full sun to half shade.
Soil: Average to rich garden soil.
Planting: Start from seed; or buy plants from nursery. Divide established plants.
Nutrients: Feed with fish emulsion.
Water: It only needs water in dry periods.
Hardiness: Tender.
Pests/diseases: Few.
Annual/perennial: Annual.

Mint (Mentha spp)

These are strong, scented herbs that spread rapidly. They have opposite leaves and white, blue, or lavender flowers. Most mints have serrated leaves. There are many varieties with a wide range of flavors.

Sun/shade: Full sun to full shade.
Soil: Rich, moist soil.
Planting: Mint can be started from seed sown in peat pots or in the seed bed, but the plants will not be ready until the

next season. Start also with plants or woody stem cuttings. The roots spread rapidly and can take over a garden bed. Confine by sinking a container of mint in the ground.

Nutrients: Feed with fish emulsion.

Water: Keep the soil moist.

Hardiness: Somewhat tender.

Pests/diseases: Few.

Annual/perennial: Perennial.

Oregano (Origanum vulgare)

The white and pink flowered varieties are favored by chefs who specialize in Mediterranean cooking. Tall oregano is a vigorous spreader. Greek and Italian oregano have the same botanical name as that of French and Wild Marjoram.

Sun/shade: Full sun.

Soil: Average to rich.

Planting: Sow the tiny seeds in the spring after the soil has warmed up to 70°F. Since seeds germinate in light, don't cover with soil. Divide the plants in the spring. Oregano grow up to $2^1/_2$ feet high. Space 12 to 24 inches apart.

Nutrients: Feed with fish emulsion.

Water: Water frequently.

Hardiness: Very hardy.

Pests/diseases: Few.

Annual/perennial: Perennial.

Parsley, Curly, (Petroselimun crispum) *and Parsley, Italian* (Petroselimun crispum, neapolitum)

Curly parsley has finely cut, tightly curled leaves. Italian parsley has a stronger flavor and flat, notched, dark green leaves.

Sun/shade: Full sun to full shade.

Soil: Rich soil.

Planting: Best started from seed. Soak the seeds in tepid water for 24 hours. Plant seeds $1/_4$ inch deep and 3 inches apart. When the plants have grown to about 6 inches, thin to stand 12 inches apart.

Nutrients: Feed regularly with fish emulsion.

Water: Keep soil moist.

Hardiness: Fairly hardy.

Pests/diseases: Leaf miners; remove the affected leaves.

Annual/perennial: Annual.

Pennyroyal (Mentha pulegium)

Another member of the mint family, pennyroyal produces dark green leaves and light purple flowered spikes. It spreads rapidly and can quickly get out of control. Use to flavor meats and sauces.

Sun/shade: Full sun to full shade.

Soil: Average garden soil.

Planting: Start with plants purchased at nursery.

Nutrients: Feed with fish emulsion.

Water: Keep soil moist.

Hardiness: Moderately hardy.

Pests/diseases: Few.

Annual/perennial: Perennial.

Rosemary (Rosmarinus officinalis)

Rosemary is an evergreen shrub with narrow, aromatic, glossy, dark green leaves. It produces clusters of small flowers that vary from pale to dark blue, pink, purple, and white. Bees love rosemary. It is an herb of many faces since it grows from upright to spreading. The leaves are widely used as a seasoning.

Sun/shade: Full sun.

Soil: Well drained.

Planting: Start from plants. Rosemary grows well in containers.

Nutrients: Feed with fish emulsion.

Water: Fairly drought resistant.

Hardiness: Hardy.

Pests/diseases: Few.

Annual/perennial: Perennial.

Sage (Salvia officinalis)

An evergreen herb with flowers in whorls or spikes. The flowers vary from white to pink to true blue. It grows to 3 feet high and 3 feet wide. The leaves are widely used to flavor meats.

Sun/shade: Full sun to half shade.

Soil: Average to poor.

Planting: Plant sage seed in the spring. You can also buy plants and set them out in early spring or start from cuttings taken during the summer. It requires 2 years to reach a usable size. Sage should be replanted every 3 or 4 years as stems become woody and tough. Thin seedlings to 20 inches apart.

Nutrients: Feed with fish emulsion.

Water: Drought-tolerant.
Hardiness: Fairly hardy.
Pests/diseases: None.
Annual/perennial: Perennial.

Savory, Summer (Satureja hortensis) and Savory, Winter (Satureja montana)

Summer savory produces whorls or white to light pink flowers and has long, narrow, mildly peppery leaves. Winter savory has stiff, narrow to oblong leaves. It has a profusion of white to lavender flowers in whorls. Winter savory has stronger flavor than summer savory.

Sun/shade: Full sun to half shade.
Soil: Average soil.
Planting: Start from seed, cuttings, or plants. Space summer savory 10 to 12 inches apart. Space winter savory 12 to 18 inches apart.
Nutrients: Feed occasionally with fish emulsion.
Water: Make sure the soil doesn't dry out, and give extra water in dry weather.
Hardiness: Hardy.
Pests/diseases: None.
Annual/perennial: Annual.

Sorrel, French (Rumex scutatus)

Sorrel has broad, ornamental, arrow-shaped, green leaves that have a lemony flavor. When it flowers, it produces a spike. It can be an attractive addition to your vegetable garden.

Sun/shade: Full sun to half shade.
Soil: Rich soil.
Planting: Sow seeds, or start from plants.
Nutrients: Fertilize with fish emulsion.
Water: Keep moist.
Hardiness: Fairly hardy.
Pests/diseases: Leaf miner; remove the affected leaves.
Annual/perennial: Perennial.

Tarragon, French (Artemesia dracunculus)

Tarragon has fine, dark green leaves with pointed tips. The leaves have a sweet, intense, licorice flavor. Use with fish, chicken, and eggs. Widely used in vinegar and sauces.

Sun/shade: Full sun to half shade.
Soil: Average.

Planting: Start by root division, or buy small plants. Space 2 feet apart. Tarragon can grow up to $2^1/_2$ feet tall.

Nutrients: Feed established tarragon in early spring and in early summer with an organic fertilizer rich in phosphorous.

Water: Keep moist.
Hardiness: Very hardy.
Pests/diseases: Few.
Annual/perennial: Perennial.

Thyme (Thymus spp)

There are many different kinds of thyme. Use with meat, soups, stews, and stuffings. Thyme is a shrublike plant that grows 8 to 12 inches high. It has slender, woody branches and tiny, gray green leaves. The flowers are produced in loose spikes.

Sun/shade: Full sun to half shade.

Soil: Average garden soil.

Planting: Sow outdoors in early spring. Start from cuttings, or buy plants. Thyme usually takes 2 years to reach usable size. Sow seeds $^1/_4$ inch deep, and thin seedlings to 12 inches apart. If you use cuttings, plant 12 inches apart.

Nutrients: Use fish emulsion occasionally.

Water: Water every 2 or 3 days in dry weather.

Hardiness: Relatively hardy.
Pests/diseases: None.
Annual/perennial: Perennial.

Verbena, Lemon (Aloysia triphylla)

Lemon Verbena is a partially evergreen, gangly herb that can grow to 6 feet tall. The narrow leaves are arranged in whorls. It produces blue flowers, and the leaves have a strong lemon aroma.

Sun/shade: Full sun to half shade.
Soil: Average.
Planting: Start from plants.
Nutrients: Use fish emulsion occasionally.

Water: Water regularly.
Hardiness: Tender.
Pests/diseases: None.
Annual/perennial: Annual.

Chapter Twelve

Bringing Vegetables and Herbs to the Table

Surprisingly, how you harvest your kitchen garden makes a tremendous difference in both freshness and flavor. Corn, for instance, holds its sweetness for only 2 to 5 days and must be picked at exactly the right time. For flavor, beets must be picked when they are small. Lettuce is most flavorful when it's picked in early morning.

Many plants go through a chemical change that converts sugar to starch. The trick is to catch them when the sugar content (the flavor) is at its peak. The general rule is to pick them when they are completely mature, and then cook them as soon as possible. This is what makes our garden-grown vegetables preferable to the supermarket vegetables; we can control when they are picked and how soon they are cooked.

Drying Vegetables

Vegetables can be dried without preservatives or salt on plastic stackable trays in an electric food dehydrator. Electric food dehydrators are available in many major retail outlets. Dehydrating removes the natural moisture from food by slowly drying it out, preventing the growth of bacteria. Dried foods are low in calories and high in nutrients. Dehydrated vegetables are great to take along on camping trips. Put them in hot water with a few of your dried herbs and presto, you have vegetable soup.

Now let's look at the individual vegetables and herbs.

Vegetables

Artichokes

Cut the individual flowers before they start to open. The smaller, more immature artichokes are the most tender. Cut artichokes darken in color once they are exposed to the air. To slow the discoloration, drop them in water fortified with 2 or 3 tablespoons of lemon juice.

To prepare whole artichokes, slice about $1/2$ inch off the tops and remove the main cluster of thorny bracts (leaves). If you want artichokes to sit upright when served, trim the stems flat with the bottoms of the bracts before cooking. Select a pan large enough to hold whole artichokes, fill the pan halfway with water, and add 1 teaspoon of salt. Cover the pan and bring to a boil. Simmer until the bottoms pierce easily.

Asparagus

Choose firm, brittle, 6- to 20-inch-tall spears that are bright green almost their entire length and have tightly closed tips. Break them off at ground level. To store, wrap the ends in a damp paper towel and refrigerate. Asparagus can be boiled, microwaved, steamed, or stir-fried.

Beans (Pole/Bush)

Green beans are ready for harvesting about 2 weeks after they bloom. Pick when the slender, crisp pods are nearly full size but the seeds are still small. Pull the pods from the plants gently to avoid uprooting bush beans or pulling vines away from their supports. Discard beans that have large seeds or swollen or limp pods. Keep plants well picked to ensure a continuous harvest and an increased yield.

Bean pods that become lumpy are no longer prime snap beans. You can let them dry and use them as dry beans. When shelled out, these are called *shelly beans*, and they are delicious.

Harvest lima bean pods when they swell yet remain green and show 3 to 4 beans per pod.

Beans (Dry/Shelling)

Pick fresh shelled beans when the seeds are fully formed and plump, but still soft. Or permit them to dry fully on the vine, and harvest them when 90 percent of the leaves have yellowed and/or fallen off and the pods are dry. Dry beans fully. Shell pods individually. Store in airtight containers.

You can reduce the cooking time for dry beans by soaking them overnight. To cook, rinse the beans, cover them with fresh water in a pan, and bring the water to a boil. Take the pan off the stove, and let it stand about 3 hours. Drain. Then use the beans in your favorite recipes.

Beets

Harvest firm, smooth-skinned beets when they are 1 to 2 inches in diameter. Pick those beets with deep green leaves. For a pickled beet treat, cook and slice 2 cups of beets. Put in glass bowl. In saucepan combine 1 cup water, 1 cup rice wine vinegar, $1/_2$ cup sugar, and $1^1/_2$ tablespoon chopped ginger. Heat until sugar is dissolved. Pour over beets. Refrigerate several hours or several days.

Broccoli

Pick broccoli while the central heads are still dark green and firm. Cut the central head on a 45-degree angle while the bud tips are still firm. After that, side shoots will develop in clusters. Some cooks use the broccoli stems extensively in all sorts of recipes. The trick is to peel the stems so they will be as tender as the flower buds.

Broccoli will keep in the refrigerator for 5 to 7 days. It must be chilled quickly. During storage it will lose Vitamin C and its stems will become tough. You can preserve broccoli by freezing it. Separate the head into bite-sized pieces, and cut the stems into 1-inch pieces. Cook the broccoli pieces in boiling water for three minutes; then plunge them into cold water for three minutes. Drain and store in plastic freezer bags. You can store frozen broccoli for up to 1 year.

Brussels Sprouts

High quality sprouts should be firm and well formed. Begin picking at the bottom. Break off a leaf below the sprout, and then remove the sprout. The upper sprouts will continue to mature as the lower ones are picked. Small, young, bright green sprouts taste best. High quality fresh sprouts will store for approximately 3 to 4 weeks at 32°F. Steamed sprouts are delicious with a mustard glaze. You can also marinate them in oil and vinegar and add them to a salad.

Cabbages

Choose firm heads that have good color. To keep the early types from bursting, harvest them promptly. Late-maturing cabbages will hold much longer. When cutting the heads from the stems, leave 2 or 3 of the wrapper leaves (outside leaves) to protect against bruising. Overmature heads are subject to splitting, especially if they are exposed to moisture fluctuations. Late-storage types will keep up to 6 months at 32°F. Early types will store 1 to 2 months. You can cook cabbage with caraway seed.

Carrots

You can use the young carrots, thinned from the carrot bed, in soups and stews. Mature carrots should be pulled when they are bright orange. This is the peak time for flavor and texture. Young carrots often haven't stored enough sugar in their roots to give them good flavor. You can leave fall carrots in the ground until you need them. Protect them, in areas where the ground freezes, with a 4-inch layer of mulch. Nutrients are stored near the skin. To preserve the nutrients, scrub carrots under running cold water with a vegetable brush, instead of peeling.

Serve carrots raw with a dip. Cooked carrots also have a wonderful flavor when topped with melted herb butter. Carrots make delicious cakes and appetizers.

Cauliflower

For peak flavor, cut the cauliflower heads from the stalk when they are compact and creamy white. They are overmature when the flower buds begin to open. If left in the garden past their prime, cauliflower heads will have a mealy texture when cooked. Serve raw cauliflower with a dip. Steam and add an herb sauce.

Celeriac (Celery Root)

Celery root is knobby and hairy, covering creamy white flesh. Pull the plants when the roots are small to medium and the tops are bright green. To prepare celeriac for cooking, scrub it with a vegetable brush. Peel the thick outer skin with a knife. Cut them into strips or cubes. To keep the peeled celeriac flesh white, submerge it in a quart of water fortified with 3 to 4 tablespoons of lemon juice.

Celery

The stalks should be crisp and ridged, with bright green leaves. In a kitchen garden, pick individual stalks as needed. The unopened flower and the tender stalks below them are particularly delicious. In mild-winter areas, many celery varieties will stand in the garden until spring, allowing light picking for soups and salads. Celery stalks stuffed with cheese make a delicious appetizer. Add raw sliced or diced celery to any dish.

Chard, Swiss

Cut individual stalks that have fresh, glossy leaves and heavy white or red stems. The stems have the crunch of celery and, some say, the taste of celery. Treat the leaves as you would spinach. Separate the leaves from the stems; slice the stems to use in salads. Add chard to soups, stir-fries, or lasagnas, or as a side dish steamed with a little butter.

Collards

Collards are hardy and usually survive to 10°F. Collards could be called a green with a bite, although they are milder than mustard greens. Start picking the tender, deep green leaves about 2 months after planting. Avoid leaves with thick, coarse veins. Discard tough stems or center ribs. Cut or tear into bite-sized pieces. Add to soups or stews, or cook with ham hocks.

Sweet Corn

Most varieties of sweet corn are ready to eat in $2\frac{1}{2}$ to 3 weeks after pollination. The hotter the weather, the quicker the corn will mature.

When corn is at its prime, the kernels will be soft and full of milk, making it very succulent. As the ear matures, the water content decreases, the sugar turns to starch, and the kernels become tough and doughy. Tough kernels indicate overmaturity.

To determine when the ears are ready, look for brown, dry silks and a round, blunt tip to the cob. If the husk fits tight to the cob, the corn is ready. If the ear is loose or soft, allow the kernels to fill out for another day or two. As a final test for sweet corn, pull back the husks of one ear and pop one of the kernels with your thumbnail. If the juice is clear, wait another day. If it is milky, the ear is ready to pick. Note that both SH2 and SE types are mature when the kernel juice is clear.

Remove the ear with a sharp downward pull, and a quick twisting wrist action. Longtime gardeners will tell you, "Don't pick the corn until the water is boiling." This isn't always practical. To retain the most flavor, store the corn in the refrigerator. You can also can or freeze corn. To freeze, blanch corn for 8 to 10 minutes and chill thoroughly in cold water. Freeze in containers or plastic freezer bags.

Popcorn

If popcorn is too dry or too wet, it won't pop properly. Let the ears dry on the stalks, and pick them when the stalks and husks are completely brown and the kernels are hard. If you can't dent the kernels with your fingernail, the popcorn is ready.

Cut small holes in a paper grocery bag, and place four or five ears inside. Hang the bag to dry for two to three weeks. When the kernels press off the cob easily, they're ready to pop.

Give popcorn a different flavor by mixing it with various spices and seasonings.

Cucumbers

Pick them when they are firm and dark green after they are about 3 to 4 inches long. The seeds get larger and harder as the fruits approach full size. Put yellowing cucumbers in the compost. Lemon cucumbers should be picked when they are 2 to 3 inches in diameter and have pale yellow skin. Keep them picked, and they will keep producing. Cut them into spears and serve with a dip. Use in salads or as a cold soup. Here's a recipe for cold cucumber soup:

> *3 medium cucumbers, peeled and sliced*
> *3 cups chicken broth*
> *$1/_4$ cup chopped onion*
> *$1/_2$ teaspoon salt*
> *1 cup half and half*
> *$1/_3$ cup sour cream*
> *2 tablespoons lemon juice*
> *$1/_4$ cup chopped fresh parsley*
> *$1/_2$ cup cucumber slices*

Combine the first four ingredients in a pan, cover, and simmer for 20 minutes. Cool. In a blender, blend until smooth. Stir in half and half, sour cream, and lemon juice. Garnish with parsley and cucumber slices.

Eggplant

Select firm, heavy fruit with taut, glossy, deeply colored skin. Purple selections should be glossy and deeply colored. White selections should be pure white, not yellowish or colored. Dull fruit is overripe and contains hard seeds.

When some eggplants are picked while small, the plants are encouraged to produce abundantly. To prepare, rinse and dry. Cut off and discard the stem. Spoon sautéed eggplant into pocket bread with other ingredients. You can also create a taste treat by sandwiching mozzarella cheese between thin slices of eggplant, then breading and frying them. For a delicious sandwich, place fried eggplant slices along with lettuce and tomato between toasted bread.

Garlic

When you can see the cloves forming in a cut open bulb, stop watering. Wait until the leaves are mostly dry, or the tops lie down in mid- to late summer, then dig up the bulbs with a

Figure 12-1a.
Braiding garlic:
Start with 3
garlic plants and
wrap the stem of
the center garlic
around the cross
stems of the
other two bulbs.

Figure 12-1b.
Add another bulb
each time you
pull an outer
stem into the
center.

Figure 12-1c.
Stop when you
have added
25–40 garlic
plants. Pull the
stems tight as the
braid dries. To
finish, wrap ends
of briad with
string.

garden fork. The heads should be closed with tight skins. To store, tie the plants in small bunches, and hang them in a cool, dark, well-ventilated location. Braiding is a great way to show off your garlic (Figures 12-1a-c).

Mince or cut the cloves into small pieces. Use as a basic ingredient in garlic butter. You can also rub uncooked cloves over a roast, or rub a raw clove inside a salad bowl before adding the salad.

To create mild-flavored garlic for cooking, roast it. The tempered bulb can be made into a pulp to impart a subtle flavor to any dish.

Horseradish

Horseradish roots should be firm. To store, wrap in a damp paper or cloth towel. Place in a plastic bag and refrigerate. Scrub, peel, and grate or cut into cubes. Horseradish will add bite to any food. Here's a recipe for fresh horseradish:

1 medium horseradish root
1 cup white vinegar
1 teaspoon salt
$^1/_2$ teaspoon sugar

Blend in a food processor. You can temper the heat by mixing in a grated potato.

Kale

Kale has beautiful, curly leaves. Begin picking individual leaves in late October to November. Look for fresh, tender leaves; avoid leaves with a thick, heavy midrib. The unopened flowers taste like the sweetest broccoli. You can boil or microwave kale. Season with an herb butter and serve.

Kohlrabi

Pick kohlrabi when the bulbs are less than 2 inches in diameter. The smaller the bulb, the more delicate the texture and flavor. Cut off the leaves, and use as a seasoning for soups. You can slice and serve kohlrabi with a dip as an appetizer. The bulbs can be hollowed out and stuffed with pork and bread crumbs.

Leeks

Dig out with a spading fork any time the leeks are 1 inch in diameter or larger. Leeks will overwinter in the ground in many areas. Harvest them before they can develop seedlings the following spring. Select those with crisp, fresh-looking, green tops. Small to medium-sized leeks (under $1^1/_2$ inches) are the most tender.

Cut off the leaf tops while still in the garden, and strip the tough outer skin from the bulb end. Spray with a hose to wash off the dirt. Put the tops and skin in the compost. Cook leeks until tender, and serve warm or chilled. You can top leeks with crumbled bacon and grated lemon peel.

Lettuce

Lettuce remains in prime eating condition for only about 3 weeks. Plant lettuce in succession so that you may enjoy fresh garden salads as much of the season as possible. Rinse greens under warm tap water to reduce bitterness. Select iceberg lettuce with fresh outer leaves. The head should give a little when squeezed. Leaf lettuce should look crisp. Put any discolored leaves in the compost. Cut out the core of iceberg lettuce. For most salads, tear leaf lettuce into bite-sized pieces. Place loose-leaf lettuce in a plastic bag, and store it in the refrigerator.

Melons

There are many types of melons. Cantaloupes are ready to eat when the stems pull off easily, usually with only a slight touch. When ripe, the rind begins to look like a corky net and turns from green to yellow or tan. The stem cracks all the way around. If cantaloupes are picked early, the fruit won't mature off the vine.

When ripe, crenshaws are medium yellow all over. The blossom end should give when pressed. When fully ripe, the green honeydew has a cream-colored rind and a fruity or honey smell. Orange honeydew rind turns from white to light salmon pink.

Juan Canary melons are ripe when the rind has turned bright yellow all over. Persian melons also have a fruity smell when ripe. The background color of the sweetest melon turns from gray green to bronze.

Judge the ripeness of the green and gold Santa Claus melon by the color of the stripes on the shell. The brighter the yellow, the riper and more flavorful the melon will be. Sharlyn melons are ripe when the background color turns from green to completely orange. Sharlyns get overripe quickly.

Season melon wedges with lemon or lime juice. You can also grill Persian melons. Here's a recipe for sweet pickled cantaloupe:

4 large firm cantaloupes
$^1/_2$ cup salt
2 quarts water
2 tablespoons whole allspice
1 tablespoon whole cloves
4 cinnamon sticks
5 cups sugar

2 cups white vinegar
2 cups water

Peel and seed cantaloupes and cut into bite-sized pieces. Dissolve salt in water. Add cantaloupe and let stand 2 hours. Drain and set aside. Tie spices in a cheesecloth bag. Combine spices and remaining ingredients in a large Dutch oven and bring to a boil. Cook 5 minutes. Add cantaloupe, return to a boil and cook 3 to 5 minutes. Remove from heat, cover, and let stand 8 hours. Remove the spice bag, and bring the syrup to a boil. Pack cantaloupe in hot, sterilized pint jars. Cover with boiling syrup, leaving $\frac{1}{2}$ inch of headspace from top of jar. Remove air bubbles; wipe jar rims. Cover at once with metal lids, and screw on bands. Process in boiling water bath for 15 minutes. Yield: 4 pints.

Mustard Greens

Regular mustard greens have a strong bite. Oriental mustard greens are milder. Pick fresh, tender green leaves, or fresh, tender plants. Shred mustard greens, and boil or microwave. Season with herb butter. Here's a recipe for mustard greens and salt pork, a staple of the Old South:

5 pounds fresh mustard greens
$\frac{1}{2}$ pound salt pork
6 to 8 cups of water
2 teaspoons bacon drippings
Green onions

Tear mustard greens into bite-sized pieces. Cut salt pork into 2-inch pieces. Combine salt pork and water in a large Dutch oven. Bring to a boil, cover, reduce heat, and simmer 30 minutes. Add mustard greens and bacon drippings. Simmer another 10 minutes. Serve with green onions.

Okra

Select small to medium pods that are deep green and firm. Trim stems and rinse, using a vegetable brush to remove the thin layer of fuzz on the stem. Cut with a sharp knife; the pods don't break or pull off easily. If you keep the pods whole, the mucilaginous juices will remain inside. Cook until tender but crisp. Slices of okra are used to thicken soups and stews. Top whole cooked okra with chives and lemon butter.

Okra is a staple vegetable in the South, and no one fries okra better than southerners. To fry okra, pick about 20 small okra pods. Soak them in buttermilk, and then roll them in flour or cornmeal. Deep-fry the okra until crisp. Yum!

Onions

When the tops begin to dry out and fall over, wait about one week to dig up the bulbs. Spread the bulbs out in the sun to cure them for a week or so to toughen the skins. Store dried onions in well-ventilated containers or in clean panty hose, tying a knot between each onion.

There are two ways to tone down the onion taste and still keep the crisp texture:

1. Immerse thin slices in ice water for about 30 minutes. They will retain some of the tanginess and remain crisp.
2. Squeeze the slices in water to break up the cells. The water will wash away some of the tanginess.

You can bake onions for a mild flavor or boil them to release the sweetness. Other choices include deep-frying slices and rings, slicing and cooking slowly, or chopping and sautéeing. You can also microwave onions. Add them to salads, soups, stews, or casseroles. There is nothing like a fresh, sliced raw onion on a hamburger.

Create a borscht by fortifying red onion soup with shredded beets. Add cream to white onion soup, and top with nutmeg and grated white cheese. Lace yellow onion soup with sherry and flavor with coriander, then top with Parmesan cheese. Here are some more tips about onions:

- Onions chopped by hand have a milder flavor than those that are chopped in a food processor. The reason is that more onion cells are bruised in a food processor, releasing compounds associated with flavor, aroma, and bitterness.
- A short cooking time over high heat releases more of these compounds; longer cooking over lower heat reduces the strong taste and brings out the natural sweetness. Too high a temperature for too long a time results in bitterness.
- Soaking in water leaches out the natural color of red onions.
- Soaking in vinegar turns a red onion a bright pink.
- Soaking in a solution of baking soda turns a red onion yellow green.

Parsnips

Harvest in late fall after the first frost. The flavor is improved by a couple of good frosts. Dig the roots anytime from October throughout the winter, as needed. Protect from freezing in the soil with a thick straw mulch.

Pull the small to medium roots. Large roots have a woody core. Add diced parsnips to soups and stews, or bake until tender. You can even use parsnips in a stir-fry.

Peas

Raw sugar snap peas make great nibbling. Snap peas are sweetest picked just before the pods fill out. Break off the ends of the snap pea, pull any strings free, and rinse well. You can serve them on a snack tray or combine them with your favorite dip. Both sugar snap and snow peas cook quickly and turn bright green. For regular peas, remove the peas from the pod, rinse, and cook.

If peas overmature, don't throw them away. Instead, treat them like beans, and add them to soups and stews. Lightly cooked peas can be added to salads.

Pea greens—the tender stems, leaves, and shoots of pea plants—have become a gourmet treat in many fine restaurants. Pop them into salads or use in stir-fries.

Peppers, Sweet

Expect 5 to 10 large bell peppers per plant. For a sweeter flavor, let your peppers ripen to maturity. It usually takes from 20 to 30 days for peppers to turn from green to red or yellow or to other colors. Cut peppers from the plants with a knife.

Bell peppers can be sliced or frozen in halves with no more than a wash to remove garden soil. You don't need to blanch peppers before freezing them. Slice all colors of peppers, and put them into a freezer bag for later use in stir-fries or spaghetti.

Peppers are great for stuffing or used as containers to show off other vegetables. Golden Bell peppers make wonderful containers for individual soufflés.

Peppers, Hot (Chilies)

Expect 20 to 50 chili peppers per plant. Pick bright, glossy peppers. Chili peppers vary from mild to hot. Anaheim and Pasilla are mild and a little bitter. In general, the smaller varieties pack the most heat. When preparing hot chili peppers, wear rubber gloves, and keep your hands away from your face. The volatile oils can cause severe burning.

Potatoes

Seventy-five days after planting, a few potatoes can be removed around the edge of each plant without threatening the main harvest. These "new potatoes" are deliciously sweet because the sugar content hasn't yet converted to starch. Use them immediately. Some cooks boil them and wrap them in bacon or sauté the little potatoes in butter.

Wait to harvest the main crop until the tops of the plants die down. Then use a pitchfork to break the small roots connecting the potatoes. Leave them for a week or two so that the skins will harden, but don't let them sit in direct sunlight. Store potatoes in a relatively dry location and at the lowest temperature possible without freezing.

Scrub the potatoes with a vegetable brush, and then peel them. To keep potatoes from discoloring, cover them with cold water before cooking. Potatoes are a great choice for microwave cooking.

Pumpkins

Choose the smaller pumpkins for eating. Pumpkin seeds baked in butter and garlic salt make a delicious snack. Cut a smaller pumpkin (2 to 3 pounds) in half and bake it at 325°F until it's tender. Peel the pumpkin pieces, and puree them in a food processor. Use the mashed pumpkin to make breads and pies.

If you scoop out the little pumpkins, you can fill them with soup and use them as individual soup bowls. Here's a recipe for seasoned pumpkin seeds:

> $^3/_4$ *cup of pumpkin seeds*
> *1 tablespoon margarine*
> $^1/_4$ *teaspoon garlic salt*
> $^1/_2$ *teaspoon Worcestershire sauce*
> $^1/_4$ *teaspoon seasoned salt*

Remove membranes from seeds; rinse and pat seeds dry. Place seeds in a pie plate, add remaining ingredients, and toss to coat all sides. Microwave at High for 8 minutes. Stir at 2-minute intervals.

Radishes

Make multiple sowings for a steady supply of radishes throughout the season. Look for bright green tops and well-formed roots. In some countries, radishes are added to soups. The green leafy tops are edible. Try mixing some, along with the radish, in salads. You can also let a few plants go to seed, and then pick the seed pods while they are immature. The pods are a crunchy addition to salads.

Oriental radishes take a little longer to mature and are a lot hotter than the regular variety.

Rhubarb

Cut the firm, crisp stalks as desired. Wash and cut the stalks into 1- or 2-inch pieces. Cook uncovered in enough water to cover the rhubarb. Sweeten with sugar to taste. Cooked rhubarb can be used in pies or served with whipped cream.

Rutabaga

Thin rutabaga in July for tasty roots by October and November. Rutabaga tastes best after a couple of good frosts. They almost always have yellow to orange skin and flesh. Peel and dice. Add to soups and stews. They can also be added to stir-fries.

Salsify

Harvest the roots in the fall. They can also be lifted and stored in damp sand for use throughout the winter, or left in the ground. Salsify has white flesh. *Scozonera* is a black-skinned relative of salsify. To keep the peeled roots white, place the roots in lemon water (3 tablespoons of lemon juice to 1 quart of water). Fry salsify, and cover it with freshly grated cheese,; or use the sharp-tasting leaves in salads.

Shallots

Dry shallots in a warm dry spot, or braid the tops and hang them out to dry. They are completely cured when the foliage loses its green color and the bulbs are papery.

Spinach

Pick only fresh, green leaves. Tear into bite-sized pieces. Raw spinach can be served with a vinaigrette or mixed with other greens. It is also used in soufflés, soups, stews, lasagna, and many other dishes. In mild-winter areas, you can grow spinach all year round.

Squash, Summer

Never plant too many summer squash, or you'll find yourself knocking on doors trying to give it away. A couple of plants go a long way. There are many types of summer squash. All have a mild, delicate flavor. Pick when the fruit is small to medium and firm with smooth skin. Never let a zucchini grow too large, or it will only be good as a club. Check plants every few days once they start to bloom.

Summer squash can be eaten raw, grilled, added to salads, or cooked in soups and stews.

Squash, Winter

Cut the vine about 1 inch from the fruit when the vine starts to dry. Allow the fruit to air cure for 7 to 10 days. To help prevent rot during storage, wipe the fruit with a solution composed of 1 teaspoon of bleach to 1 quart of water. Store at 45° to 60°F. The best squash have a hard, thick shell and feel heavy for their size.

Winter squash can be used in many different dishes, including pies, soups, stews, or baked casseroles.

Sweet potatoes

When we grew these, we were delighted with the results. The taste was sweet and delicious. You can also root the tops in jars of water placed under your sink or in another dark spot.

Sweet potatoes can be boiled, baked, or added to other dishes. Sliced thin, they can be fried or baked in the oven as potato chips.

Tomatoes

Pick smooth, well-formed tomatoes that are heavy for their size. There is nothing like the taste of a vine-ripened tomato. The larger tomatoes are great stuffed. Scoop out the pulp and leave the shells intact. Cut scalloped edges around the tomato, and add crab and avocado, turkey and dill, or a variety of cooked vegetables.

You can also ripen green tomatoes at the end of the season by wrapping individual tomatoes in newspaper and placing them in a cardboard box, or by storing them on a drying rack in a cool basement. Tomatoes ripen at different rates.

Turnips

Pick turnips when they are young and tender. The tastiest roots are $1^1/_2$ to 2 inches in diameter. The larger they are, the tougher they will be. Turnips are good sliced raw or added to soups and stews. Turnips can be peeled, boiled, and mashed like potatoes for a tasty side dish. The turnip tops (called greens) can be harvested at any size.

Watermelon

A watermelon is ready to harvest when the fruit is uniform in shape and the stem end slips off easily. If there are small blotchy spots around the stem end, it means the melon is very sweet. When ripe, the skin on the bottom of the melon turns from white to yellow. And the thump test? Hold the melon in one hand, and thump it; if you feel a vibration in the hand holding the melon, it's a full, solid melon.

Herbs

Herbs brighten up the simplest meal or provide the finishing touch to fine cuisine. The bold flavors of herbs can replace salt or fat in some recipes and can permeate cooked dishes to add an extra dimension.

When snipped frequently, herbs respond with renewed vigor. Any excess should be dried or frozen (Figure 12-2). To enhance a dinner meal, place a bouquet of fresh herbs in the middle of the table. The aroma will fill the entire room.

Tie together sprigs of oregano, rosemary, and sage, and use them like a pastry brush to apply marinade for barbecuing.

Dried herbs can be made into herbal wreaths. Pick an assortment of herbs, such as dark green mints, Italian parsley, purple opal basil, variegated sage, and other basils. Dry the herbs, and gather them into bundles of 5 to 7 stems, cut about 5 inches long. Using glue or pins, attach the bundles to a straw base from a craft store. Alternate any contrasting colors. Overlap the leaves to cover the stems, working from the inner edge to the outer edge. You can also add dried flowers if you like.

Herbs can be added to vinegars and sugars. To make a white wine herb vinegar, fill a glass jar with fresh herb sprigs. Use rosemary, thyme, or basil by itself, or combine several herbs, such as lemon thyme, marjoram, and oregano. Fill the jar with white wine, secure the lid, and let it stand at room temperature for several weeks. Strain the mixture through cheesecloth. Use the vinegar as desired.

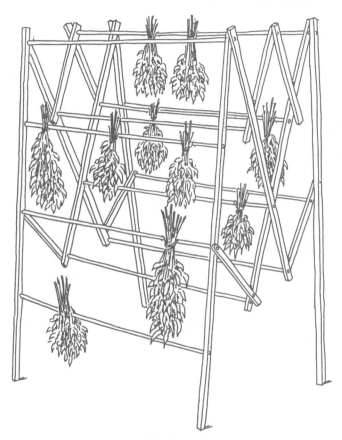

Figure 12-2. Drying herbs.

You can also buy a fancy vinegar jar, add a fresh sprig of your favorite herb, and fill the jar with the strained vinegar. Add a bow, and give the jar as a delightful gift.

Seed sources for many herbs are included in the previous text or listed here.

Anise

Harvest the seeds about one month after the flowers bloom, when they turn gray brown, by clipping them into a paper bag. Use the fresh leaves to spice up a green salad, or in soups, stews, and sauces. Seed source: ABU ALL COM DEG GOU GUR HEN JUN LED LEJ MEY NIC PIN POR RIC SOU STO TAY TER TIL VER WIL WILL

Balm, Lemon

Harvest the leaves anytime during the season. You can cut the plant back to within 2 to 4 inches of the ground, and it will regrow the following year. You can dry the leaves for use during the winter. The aroma of lemon balm becomes faint when it's dried. Use the fresh heart-shaped leaves in teas, salads, soups, and stews. Bees love this plant. Seed source: BOU BURP COM DAB GOU GUR HEN HIG JOH JUN LEJ NIC ORN PAR PIN POR RED RIC SHE SEE SOU STO TAY VER WILL

Basil

Gather basil leaves before they bloom or when blooming begins. Pinch the top third of the basil plant regularly. Dry the leaves in a paper grocery bag with holes cut in the sides for ventilation. Hang the bag if possible. This drying process takes about 2 weeks. Store the leaves in an airtight container away from direct sunlight. Basil may also be preserved by freezing the leaves and stems, or by pureeing the leaves and freezing them. Try chopping fresh basil and adding it to spaghetti sauce. It adds a wonderful flavor to chicken, fish, pasta dishes, and vegetables.

Bergamot (Bee Balm)

Bergamot has citrus-scented leaves and flowers. Both can be used in salads or teas. Lemon Bergamot leaves were used by Hopi Indians to flavor wild game. Seed source: NIC RIC VER

Borage

Clip leaves before the buds flower. Use the blossoms to decorate beverages, and use fresh chopped leaves in salads and summer drinks. Seed source: ALL ABU BOU BURP BURR COM COO DEG GAR GOU HIG JLH JOH JUN LEJ LED LIB MEY NIC PAR PIN POR RED RIC SEE SOU STO TAY TER TWI VER WILL

Burnet Salad

This herb has nutty, cucumber-flavored leaves that are used in dressings, salads, casseroles, vinegars, cream cheeses, and soups. Seed source: BOU COM DEG GOU NIC PAR RED RIC SEE SOU TAY VER

Chervil

Pick leaves just before buds break. Green tender leaves may be cut and dried. To harvest, clip whole plants before they flower, and hang them upside down in a shady location. Chervil has a mild licorice or tarragon-like flavor and can be used in every dish in which parsley is used. Seed source: ABU ALL BOU COM DEG GAR JLH LED NIC PIN POR SEE SHE STO TAY TER TIL

Chives

Chives are an essential culinary herb. Clip the leaves with scissors. Use the leaves fresh or frozen. Chives lose their flavor quickly and don't dry well, but they can be chopped and frozen in a plastic bag. Make up an herb seasoning for omelettes, creamy sauces, and salads by mixing chopped parsley, chives, marjoram, and thyme.

Cilantro/Coriander

Harvest plants when they are 6 inches high by clipping the leaves. You can dry the leaves in a paper bag and store them in an airtight container. Use fresh or dried, and add the seeds to many dishes. If you let the plant go to seed, gather the seeds as they ripen in mid-summer.

Dill

Pick fresh leaves as soon as the flowers begin to open. Harvest leaves early in the day before the plant begins to set its flower buds. Snip the leaves close to the stem. Cover seed stalks with a plastic bag, close the bag loosely, and collect the seeds as they ripen. Some cooks grind the dill seeds into a powder. You can also freeze the stems and snip off the leaves as you need them. Dill has a robust flavor that adds life to potatoes, eggs, cream cheese, dips, pickles, and carrots. It also gives an aromatic flavor to salmon, salads, soups, and stews. When you use fresh dill, add it near the end of cooking so that it retains its sharp flavor. Seed source: ABU ALL BOU BURP COM FAR GUR HEN HIG LED MEY NIC ORG PAR PIN POR RED RIC SEE SOU STO TAY WIL

Fennel

Pick the stems just before the flower blooms. Pick the leaves when the flowers start to bloom and as soon as they are large enough. You can chop and freeze them in plastic bags. They add a slightly licorice flavor to salads. The seeds are ready to harvest when they are hard and turn from green to brown. Pick them before they get scattered, and finish drying them indoors. They add a unique taste to baked breads, cakes, and cookies. They also brighten up fish, meat, cheese, and vegetable dishes.

Hyssop

Hyssop is a decorative plant with slightly bitter leaves. The leaves are used in salads, game meat, soups, and stews. Pick before they flower. Seed source: ABU BOU COM DAB DEG GAR GOU LEJ NIC ORN PIN RIC SEE SEED SOU TAY TER WILL

Lovage

Lovage resembles a giant celery plant; even the flavor resembles celery. Lovage is used in tea, meat, fish, and vegetable dishes. Pick before they flower. Seed source: ABU BOU COM DEG GAR GOU HEN JOH LEJ NIC PAR PIN SEED SOU TAY TER VER WILL

Marjoram, Sweet

Trim off the ball-shaped flower clusters before they bloom, or remove sprigs as needed. Marjoram adds flavor to chicken, cheese, and vegetables.

Mint

The more frequently you cut the sprigs, the better mint will grow. Fresh mint is best, and young leaves are more flavorful than older ones. Many cooks use mint as a garnish or in jellies. There are many kinds of mint, and each complements a beverage, cottage cheese, potatoes, or vegetables. Choose your flavor! You can freeze or dry mint.

Oregano

You can start harvesting sprigs of oregano when the plants are 6 inches high. Use fresh leaves as needed. Leaves may also be preserved by drying; just hang them in bunches. Cretan, Greek, and Syrian varieties have the strongest flavors. Sicilian and Italian types are milder. The leaves add an aromatic, if somewhat minty, flavor to tomato dishes.

Parsley

Pick mature leaves from first-year plants. Harvest leaves from second-year plants before the flowers bloom. You can dry by hanging the whole plant in a shady, well-ventilated area. Crumble when dry, and store in airtight containers. It has an even better flavor if you chop it up and freeze it. Toss chopped parsley into salads, soups, casseroles, and vegetables. Parsley has a strong flavor that can enhance almost any food. It is famous as a garnish.

Perilla (Shiso)

This herb is highly prized for Oriental dishes. Green Perilla (Aoshiso) is the preferred variety for sushi. Purple Perilla (Akahisho) is preferred for pickling. Red Perilla (Red Shiso) leaves are used in salads and soups and as a garnish for fish. Pick in all seasons. Seed source: GOU JOH NIC ORN SEE SEED SOU SUN THE VER

Rosemary

Pick after the morning dew has dried but before the sun can leach out the essential oils that keep herbs fresh and flavorful. Rosemary is the star of many Mediterranean-style dishes. Use fresh or dried. Dry by hanging or placing in a paper bag that has holes cut around the sides. Drying takes about two weeks.

Sage

Sage leaves can be used fresh or dried. Pick leaves as soon as they are large enough to handle, and dry them on a tray. Then store them away from light. There are many varieties that flavor meats, dressings, and sauces. Most sages can be grown in pots inside or out. Pinch back to keep bushy.

Summer Savory

Summer savory is preferred most for culinary use. Gather leaves from prebloom until bloom. Lemon savory has an intense lemon scent. Seed source: ABU ALL BOU BURP BURR COM DEG GAR GOU JOH JUN LEJ LIB MEY NIC ORG ORN PAR RIC SEE SEED SHE SOU TAY TER TIL TWI VER WIL

Tarragon

The leaves are most flavorful when picked prebloom or just before blooming begins. Preserve tarragon by drying. French tarragon makes a good green sauce and is the true tarragon, but it doesn't propagate by seeds. The anise-flavored leaves of Mexican tarragon (also called sweet mace) are narrow, glossy, green, and serrated. They are used extensively in Mexican dishes.

Use tarragon in mayonnaise, butter, white wine vinegar, and vegetables.

Thyme

Harvest heavily just before the bloom, and pinch off sprigs as needed up to 6 weeks before the first fall frost. Clip the tops of plants when in full bloom. Orange balsam thyme has an orange flavor and is well suited to fruit salads. Other varieties have the scent and flavor of nutmeg, caraway, and lemon. Thyme is excellent in soups, sauces, and breads. Seed source: DAB RIC.

Seed Catalog Sources

COO The Cook's Garden
PO Box 535
Londonderry, VT 05148
Order: 802/824-3400

DAB Dabney Herbs
PO Box 22061
Louisville, KY 40252
Order: 502/893-5198

DEG DeGiorgi Seed Co.
6011 N Street
Omaha, NE 68117-1634
Order: 800/858-2480

FAR Farmer Seed and Nursery
1706 Morrissey Drive
Bloomington, IL 61704
Order: 507/334-1623

FIS Fisher's Seeds
PO Box 236
Belgrade, MT 59714
Order: 406/388-6052

GAR Garden City Seeds
1324 Red Crow Road
Victor, MT 59875-9713
Order: 406/961-4837

GLE Glecker's Seedmen
Metamora, OH 43540

GOU The Gourmet Gardener
8650 College Boulevard
Overland Park, KS 66210
Order: 913/345-0490

GUR Gurney's Seed & Nursery Co.
110 Capital Street
Yankton, SD 57079
Order: 605/665-1930

HEN Henry Field's Seed & Nursery
Co.
415 North Burnett
Shenandoah, IA 51602
Order: 605/665-9391

HIG High Altitude Gardens
PO Box 1048
Hailey, ID 83333
Order: 208/788-4363

HOR Horticultural Enterprises
PO Box 810082
Dallas, TX 75381-0082

<u>CODE</u>

PLA Plants of the Southwest
     Route 6, PO Box 11A
     Santa Fe, NM 87501
     Order: 505/471-2212

PON Pony Creek Nursery
     PO Box 16
     Tilleda, WI 54978
     Order: 715/787-3889

POR Porter & Son, Seedmen
     PO Box 104
     Stephenville, TX 76401-0104

RED The Redwood City Seed Co.
     PO Box 361
     Redwood City, CA 94064
     Order: 415/325-SEED

RIC Richters
     Goodwood, Ontario, Canada
     L0C 1A0
     Order: 905/640-6677

ROS Roswell Seed Co.
     PO Box 725
     Roswell, NM 88202
     Order: 505/662-7701

<u>CODE</u>

SEE Seeds Blum
     Idaho City Stage
     Boise, ID 83706

SEED Seeds of Change
     PO Box 15700
     Santa Fe, NM 87506-5700

SHE Shepherd's Garden Seeds
     6116 Highway 9
     Felton, CA 95018
     Order: 408/335-6910

SOU Southern Exposure Seed
     Exchange
     PO Box 170
     Earlysville, VA 22936
     Order: 804/973-4703

STO Stokes
     PO Box 548
     Buffalo, NY 14240-0548
     Order: 716/695-6980

SUN Sunrise Enterprises
     PO Box 330058
     West Hartford, CT 06133-0058

TAY Taylor's Herb Garden
1535 Lone Oak Road
Vista, CA 92084
Order: 619/727-3485
Fax: 619/727-0289

TER Territorial Seed Co.
20 Palmer Avenue
Cottage Grove, OR 97424
Order: 503/942-9547

THE The Good Earth Seed Co.
PO Box 5644
Redwood City, CA 94063

THO Thompson & Morgan Inc.
PO Box 1308
Jackson, NJ 08527-0308
Order: 800/274-7333

TIL Tillinghast Seed Co.
PO Box 738
La Conner, WA 98257
Order: 206/466-3329

TOM The Tomato Seed Co. Etc.
PO Box 1400
Tryon, NC 28782

TOMA Tomato Growers Supply Co.
PO Box 2237
Fort Myers, FL 33902

TWI Otis S. Twilley Seed Co., Inc.
PO Box 65
Trevose, PA 19053
Order: 800/622-7333

VER Vermont Bean Seed Co.
PO Box 250
Fair Haven, VT 05743
Order: 802/273-3400

WIL Willhite Seed Co.
Poolville, TX 76487
Order: 800/828-1840

WILL William Dam Seeds
PO Box 8400
Dundas, Ontario
Canada L9H 6M1
Order: 905/628-6641

Index

Page numbers in *italics* indicate illustrations or tables.